TAX SHIFT

How to Help the Economy, Improve the Environment, and Get the Tax Man off Our Backs

Alan Thein Durning
Yoram Bauman

With research assistance by
Rachel Gussett
Erik Haunreiter
David Kershner
Bill McKee
Jennifer Tice

Illustrated by
Don Baker

NEW Report No. 7
April 1998

Northwest Environment Watch
Seattle, Washington

NEW thanks editor and typesetter Ellen W. Chu and reviewers Jeff Allen, Gardner Brown, Cathy Caruthers, Ralph Cipriani, Cliff Cobb, Chris Hagerbaumer, M. Jeff Hamond, Jane Koenig, Bill Pease, David Pimentel, Dave Robison, David Roodman, Paul Sabin, the Skujas, Anne N. Solwick, Nic Warmenhoven, and Bridget Wieghart for their skilled contributions. We also thank for their dedicated assistance interns Carolyn Beaver, Patrick McMahon, and Frana Milan and volunteers David Ahlers, Esra Basak, Peter Carlin, Mark Cliggett, Chris Cramer, Owen Hamel, Norman Kunkel, Kirk Larsen, Jason Randles, Chris Rothfuss, Marilyn Roy, Erik Schweighofer, John Wedgwood, and Darrel Weiss. NEW is grateful to its board of directors: Lester R. Brown of Washington, D.C.; Sandi Chamberlain of Victoria, B.C.; Aaron Contorer of Kirkland, Wash.; Alan Thein Durning of Seattle; Jeff Hallberg of Kirkland, Wash.; Sandra Blair Hernshaw of Seattle; Tyree Scott of Seattle; and Rosita Worl of Juneau.

Financial support for this book was provided by the Nathan Cummings Foundation, Ford Foundation, and other contributors to Northwest Environment Watch. These include more than 1,600 individuals and the Brainerd Foundation, Bullitt Foundation, C. S. Fund, William and Flora Hewlett Foundation, Lazar Foundation, Merck Family Fund, True North Foundation, and Turner Foundation. Views expressed are the authors' and do not necessarily represent those of Northwest Environment Watch or its directors, officers, staff, or funders. Northwest Environment Watch is a 501(c)(3) tax-exempt organization.

This book was printed by Artcraft Printing Company, Seattle, Washington, with vegetable-based ink on recycled paper (second printing). Text, 100 percent postconsumer waste; cover, 35 percent preconsumer and 15 percent postconsumer waste; both bleached without chlorine.

Excerpts from this book may be printed in periodicals with written permission from Northwest Environment Watch, a 501(c)(3) tax-exempt organization. To learn more, contact:

Northwest Environment Watch ,1402 Third Avenue, Suite 500
Seattle, WA 98101-2130 USA; (206) 447-1880; fax (206) 447-2270
new@northwestwatch.org; www.northwestwatch.org

TABLE OF CONTENTS

WHAT WE'VE GOT

E ver since the Boston Tea Party—which was, after all, about taxes, not tea—tax revolts have shaped politics on this continent. No wonder. Taxes not only claim billions of dollars from citizens; they also influence billions of daily decisions—shaping, or misshaping, the economy.

In general, economics tells us that when you tax something, you get less of it. Our problem is that we tax things we want more of, such as paychecks and enterprise, instead of things we want less of, such as toxic waste and resource depletion. Naturally, we get less money and more messes. *Tax Shift* is about doing the opposite—removing taxes from "goods" and putting them on "bads." This book is not about raising or lowering taxes overall. Whether you think government is too big, too small, or just right, tax shifting is a revolt that makes sense: it gets taxes off our backs and onto our side.

A tax shift would allow us to reduce or eliminate many existing taxes: regressive property, payroll, and sales taxes that are hardest on the lower and middle classes; enterprise-killing business taxes; even the mind-boggling personal income tax. Instead, by building on a rudimentary framework of existing minor levies, we could tax actions that corrode the public good. We could tax emissions of deadly fine particles, greenhouse gases, and other air pollutants; discharges of toxic heavy metals and other water pollutants; and the manufacture and use of pesticides and other hazardous chemicals. We could tax away most traffic jams, by charging drivers for use of major routes at rush hour. We could protect natural ecosystems by taxing the pumping of fresh water, the impounding of rivers behind dams, and the felling of virgin timber. Finally, by moving the weight of the property tax off buildings and onto urban land values, we could promote the growth of compact, walkable neighborhoods and slow the creep of our suburbs into farms and forests.

Shifting the tax burden would send out powerful signals—signals that would reorient consumption and pro-

Dear Reader,

Merely reading the words *tax* and *policy* in the same sentence can cause a person's eyes to glaze. We've tried to keep things interesting, but if your eyes do glaze, just remember what's at stake: the environment, the economy, and—if you're part of an average northwestern household— almost $20,000 in all forms of taxes each year.[1] (We use the word *taxes* in connection with all policies that generate government funds. For the sake of variety or historical accuracy, though, we will occasionally call them levies or charges.)

Read on. A tax shift might save you a bundle.

duction in our homes and businesses. Tax shifting would harness the profit motive for environmental ends and wring out the waste of resources. Governments would still get their money, and—because taxes on "bads" do not bog down the economy as much as many existing taxes on "goods"— employment levels and incomes would rise.

In economic terms, a tax shift would take taxes off labor and capital and put them on the third factor of production—resources, the gifts of nature. Labor refers to people working. Capital means physical objects created by people, such as buildings, tools, and machinery. The gifts of nature are resources not made by people, such as air, forests, fossil fuels, land, metals, water, a stable climate, and rivers and other habitats. Taxing labor and capital tells businesses and households to scrimp on workers and tools—in other words, to practice underemployment and underinvestment. Taxing the gifts of nature (or, more precisely, taxing actions that degrade the gifts of nature) tells people to conserve these gifts.

Taxes on resources correct one of the most glaring flaws of market economies: blindness to environmental costs. Failure to charge for the use of the atmosphere as a receptacle for poisonous gases, for example, results in too much air pollution. Failure to charge for the disruption of watersheds results in too many floods. Yet for individual firms, there is no place in the ledger for the environmental costs of production that fall on others—costs such as damage of a worker's DNA that causes disease decades later, the draining of a wetland that offers wildlife habitat, or the release of toxic substances so mobile they eventually permeate the breast milk of women in the Arctic. Environ-

mental taxes put these costs—or at least crude monetary
approximations of them—on the books.

The prospect of aiding both economy and environment has sparked modest tax shifts in the Netherlands,
Spain, the United Kingdom, and three Scandinavian countries since 1991. In North America, this trend has yet to
take hold. The history of tax politics on this continent
suggests that adopting a reform for the first time in the
first place is harder than spreading it to ten others, so road
testing a tax shift on this side of the Atlantic could quickly
set off similar reforms across the United States and Canada.[2]

This book attends to one possible test plot—the Pacific Northwest, defined as the region whose rivers run
into the Pacific Ocean through North America's temper-
ate rain forests. Home to 15 million people, this region
stretches from Alaska's Prince William Sound to the red-
wood coast of California and inland to headwaters as far
east as the Rocky Mountains. More than twice the size of
Texas, it encompasses British Columbia, Idaho, Oregon,
and Washington, along with neighboring parts of Alaska,
California, and Montana (see map inside front cover). The
region combines traditions of political innovation and
environmental conservation.

In the Northwest, taxes claimed $107 billion in 1996,
one-third of the gross regional product. (When we report
data for the Northwest as a whole in this book, we exclude the states only partially within the region.) Some
$89 billion of that money came from taxes on labor and
capital, mostly in the form of payroll taxes, personal income taxes, corporate income and other business taxes,
and sales and property taxes. Just 17 percent of revenue

collected came from taxes on resources. The largest of these were the part of the property tax that falls on land, rather than on buildings, and the gas tax. Others included health-oriented taxes on alcohol and tobacco, small energy taxes, pollution taxes, and motor vehicle fees. Elsewhere in the tax codes, meanwhile, environmentally damaging activi-

Taxing Logic?

Combined tax rate on each dollar of take-home pay for a middle-income Oregon family 31%

Tax rate on each dollar spent on pesticides in Oregon 0%

Combined tax rate on profits of major service businesses in British Columbia 46%

Average tax on each of the 2.8 billion pounds of industrial air and water pollutants emitted annually in B.C. .... 0.3¢

Washington business tax rate on each dollar received by a public or nonprofit hospital 1.5%

Washington business tax rate on each dollar received by a nuclear fuel manufacturer 0.275%

Share of income a poor California family pays in state and local taxes 12%

Tax rate on old-growth timber cut in California 3%

Sources: see note 3.

ties including driving, logging, and mining received special subsidies. (NEW describes these subsidies in a companion volume, *Hazardous Handouts: Taxpayer Subsidies to Environmental Destruction*. See inside back cover.)[4]

Because taxes on labor and capital are high in the Northwest as elsewhere, the prices of housing and labor are higher than they should be. So are the prices of things that use labor intensively, such as medical care and education. In both the United States and Canada, the combination of income taxes and payroll taxes (such as unemployment insurance) puts a tax burden on paychecks that usually exceeds 30 percent. For a worker to get $1,000 in after-tax pay, she and her employer must write checks worth $300 or more to the government. These taxes effectively penalize hiring and working and push the economy to use fewer workers instead of fewer natural resources.[5]

Levies on capital and labor squelch investment and worker effort. Every dollar raised through taxes on capital or labor reduces economic output by dampening productivity. Overall, taxes affecting the Northwest cause so-called deadweight losses of about 24 cents per dollar collected. All together, these losses come to approximately $26 billion annually in the region, equal to 8 percent of economic output.[6]

A tax shift revolt in the Northwest may not come easily. The idea is still new and unfamiliar; existing taxes, though products of a history of errors, have the force of custom behind them. Fortunately, reforms need not occur all at once. A tax shift can proceed in steps, and each step will strengthen the economy while helping the environment. In the end, the practical challenge is one of public educa-

Death and Taxes

Air and water pollution and other environmental contaminants killed at least 3,400
people, possibly three times as many, in the
Pacific Northwest in 1996. Motor vehicles—
the worst air polluters—killed another 1,991 in crashes. (Some
253 of them were pedestrians.) Smoking killed about 21,400.
Some 5,800 people died from alcohol consumption.[7]

These figures are based on statistics. We cannot pick out all
the victims' names from the list of the 106,923 people—2,248
of them children—who died in the Northwest in 1996. But the
best available evidence suggests that 31,800 did die of these
less-than-natural causes and that for every person who died,
many more were maimed, handicapped, or sickened.[8]

A tax shift that discouraged polluting, driving, smoking,
and drinking would have saved some of these lives. So in a
way, the existing tax system—by failing to penalize dangerous
acts—is implicated in these deaths. Tax policy's sin is one of
omission, not commission, but the victims are just as dead.
This unexpected collusion of the tax man and the grim reaper
adds a sinister new twist to Benjamin Franklin's old observa-
tion, "Nothing in this world is certain but death and taxes."[9]

tion and political organizing, and the organizing may come
more easily than expected. After all, we have much to lose—
needless death and suffering, unnecessary poverty and unemployment, endangerment of the landscape, and tax laws
that punish virtues while rewarding vices.

Idaho Jones and the Taxes of Doom

Meet Idaho Jones and his sisters: British Columbia Jones, Oregon Jones, and Washington Jones. They aren't real people, of course. But they could be. They are statistically average representatives of the Northwest in general and of their state or province in particular. Now approaching his thirty-third birthday, Idaho Jones is the baby of the family. B.C. and Oregon Jones are the eldest at 36. Washington is 34. (Half the people in each state or province are older than the Jones namesake; half are younger.) All are married and have one child (except for B.C., who has two). Idaho and his wife have a ten-year-old named Jessica—the most popular baby name in the year of her birth. A rarity, Idaho was born in the state where he lives now; the other Joneses take after their parents, who moved around a lot.[10]

The Jones family finances are, well, average. Idaho and his wife earn $40,500 a year—the state's median household income for non-elderly married couples. Oregon and Washington have household incomes in the mid- to high 40s. B.C. Jones and her husband earn Can$55,000 (about US$40,000). The Joneses don't get to spend all that money, though. In addition to federal income and payroll taxes, the Jones siblings pay about 10 percent of their household incomes in state, provincial, and local taxes. Those $3,000–$6,000 disappear in different ways: Oregon Jones, for instance, pays state income tax but no sales tax, while Washington does the opposite. In exploring the often murky labyrinth of tax policies in the Northwest, we'll ask the Joneses to help us keep up with how taxes affect "average" northwesterners.[11]

How We Got It

How we collect revenue is an accident of history springing from a history of accidents. Even a cursory review debunks the notion that very much sustains the present regime besides force of habit. It also uncovers valuable lessons for would-be tax shifters.

Our tax laws were cobbled together through a century and a half of political compromises and special pleading. They are revealing maps of past convenience and vulnerability: when revenues were needed, legislators sought the most convenient means of extracting funds, which usually meant dunning those least able to resist. As Louis XIV's financial advisor, Jean Baptiste Colbert, once said, "The art of taxation consists in so plucking the goose as to obtain the largest possible amount of feathers with the smallest possible amount of hissing." Big changes have come largely during times of crisis, and even then voters have usually cast tax ballots based on perceptions of their own immediate self-interest. Equally important, tax policy rests on custom. People have mostly accepted what they were used to, so politicians tell one another, "The best tax is an old tax."[12]

The end point of this ad hoc process is a tax system with only one coherent goal: capturing money. It took in

$107 billion in 1996, one-third of the region's economic output. National governments received 62 percent of the total revenue collected in the Northwest, most of it from personal income taxes, with corporate income taxes and payroll taxes making up almost all the remainder. States and provinces collected about one-quarter, most of it from income and sales taxes. Localities collected the remaining 15 percent, mostly from property taxes. Northwest jurisdictions generate revenue differently: Oregon and Montana leave sales untaxed, for example, while Washington and Alaska do not tax personal income (see Appendix for details). But these differences are overwhelmed by the similarities: all governments in the Northwest fund themselves by taxing beneficial activities ("goods") rather than harmful ones ("bads").[13]

The incessant complexification of tax policy, mostly driven by legislators placating special interests, has yielded a body of law that is virtually impenetrable—literally, a tax *code*. The original text of U.S. income tax law was 14 pages long. Its current incarnation, the Internal Revenue Code, is 7.5 million words long and takes up six inches of shelf space. The regulations that interpret it take up another foot.[14]

Canada's tax code is no less gargantuan, and subsidiary governments—states and provinces especially, but also counties, cities, school districts, port districts, utility districts, and others—pile on taxes of their own. British Columbia alone has 543 separate units of local government; Washington has 1,709. A collection of all the Northwest's tax rules would fill a small library.[15]

Aside from the tax collectors themselves, few people actually understand tax law. Half a million accountants and

How to Tell a Good Tax from a Bad Tax

We evaluate taxes on the basis of four criteria:

Economy: Does the tax encourage or discourage enterprise, growth in productivity, and job creation? Specifically, does the tax cause what economists call a "deadweight loss": a loss of economic output caused by distorted incentives created by the tax? Taxes on wages, for example, discourage people from working. Taxes on investment discourage people from investing. Both reduce economic output.

Equity: Does the tax fall on people in proportion to their ability to pay? Progressive taxation attempts to equalize sacrifice instead of simple percentages by taking a larger proportion of income from higher-income households than from poorer ones. Regressive taxes, by contrast, take a larger share of income from middle-class and poor households than from affluent ones. Because the cost of some taxes is passed on from the initial taxpayer to others, assessing fairness requires paying attention to who ultimately feels the tax bite.

Environment: Does the tax encourage or discourage resource conservation and pollution prevention? Does the tax correct the failure of the market to reflect environmental costs, such as pollution's effects on human health?

Ease of administration: Is the tax easy to administer and enforce? Is it easy for taxpayers to comply with the tax? Is it easy to evade?

lawyers are kept busy just interpreting U.S. tax policy for the public; most of us have only a tentative grasp on the subject. Perhaps consequently, political debate focuses almost entirely on *how much* to tax, rather than on *what* to tax.[16]

A History of Accidents

The major features of the apparatus that gathers government revenue are relics of earlier tax reforms. In 1910, most national revenue collected in the Pacific Northwest came from tariffs—customs duties—while most revenue collected by states, provinces, and localities came from property taxes and public sales of natural resources. By 1940, everything had changed. Most national revenue came from taxes on personal income and corporate profit, and most state and provincial income came from taxes on income, profit, and sales.[17] **Lesson 1. Nothing about taxes is preordained.**

The national personal income taxes in both Canada and the United States trace their origins to farmers' opposition to high tariffs. Indeed, when the Populist Movement of the late nineteenth century won passage of a federal income tax in the United States in 1894, the tax was designed to replace regressive tariff revenue. The Supreme Court promptly ruled the tax unconstitutional, but by 1909—with the Populists largely vanquished—the movement's favored tax had become a mainstream idea. Democrats in Congress, allied with a few farm state Republicans such as William Borah of Idaho, proposed a federal income tax anew. An epic political battle with the White House ensued, and when the dust cleared, the nation found itself with a tax no one had previously asked for—the corporate income tax—but no personal income tax.[18]

Personal Income Taxes

U.S. and Canadian federal governments depend on personal income taxes for almost half their revenue. B.C., Idaho, and Oregon also depend heavily on them. Washington and Alaska have no personal income tax. (For details, see Appendix.)

Economy: Income taxes are a heavy drag on the economy. Each dollar collected by national government results in a deadweight loss of about 31 cents; state and provincial taxes cause larger losses.[19]

Equity: Income taxes are among the most progressive taxes, despite countless exemptions that erode fairness. A flaw, though, is that income taxes focus on cash flow—what is earned yearly—rather than wealth, which determines ability to pay.

Environment: Income taxes fall heavily on paychecks, discouraging people from working and increasing the true cost of labor to businesses. Firms therefore focus on conserving labor rather than on conserving resources. Furthermore, numerous loopholes reduce the tax burden on income from nonlabor sources in general, such as investments, and from a variety of environmentally destructive activities in particular.

Ease of administration: Complying takes Americans 5 billion hours each year. For every dollar raised, U.S. taxpayers spend nine cents obeying the law. Cheating is widespread: roughly one-fifth of income goes unreported.[20]

Our grade: D   Your grade: _____

Only four years later, after state legislatures had ratified an amendment to the constitution, did the personal income tax come into being. Apparently, the states ratified the constitutional amendment because legislators thought the tax would fall mostly on capitalists in a few eastern cities. Oregon and Washington ratified it with virtually no dissent; in Washington, the amendment's passage went almost unmentioned in the local press.[21]

Considering what the personal and corporate income taxes would later become, they had modest beginnings. The personal income tax passed as a brief amendment to an act reforming tariffs. Indeed, the Bureau of Internal Revenue it created was so named to distinguish income taxes from the larger sums of "external revenues"—tariffs. At first, both new taxes were minor obligations, paid only by a few, but they grew fast. By 1920, income taxes dominated the nation's revenue stream, though they still touched relatively few northwesterners. Scarcely 10 percent of residents of Washington State filed personal returns that year. Congress expanded the tax explosively during World War II; the number of filers soared from 4 million in 1939 to 43 million in 1945.[22] **Lesson 2. Think big, start small.**

North of the forty-ninth parallel, events followed a similar course. Canadian finance ministers have long written their proposals with U.S. tax laws close at hand because Canada competes with its larger neighbor for immigrants and capital. Thus, Canadian leaders had always spoken in adamant opposition to taxing personal income before the United States began doing so in 1913. But in 1917, confronted with the rising cost of World War I, Canada enacted an income tax much like America's.[23]

Payroll Taxes

Payroll taxes generate 36 percent of federal revenue in the United States and 15 percent in Canada. U.S. payroll taxes for Social Security, Medicare, and unemployment insurance come to more than 15 percent of pay. Canada's payroll taxes for unemployment insurance and the Canada Pension Plan are almost as high and set to rise higher. Both countries are preparing for the baby boomers' retirement by collecting more payroll tax than they need now. Canada invests the surplus. The United States lends the surplus to the Treasury at low interest rates, then spends it on the general functions of government.[24]

Economy: Payroll taxes have deadweight losses of about 26 cents per dollar of revenue and hit small businesses hard.[25]

Equity: Payroll taxes are extremely regressive. They are actually graduated in reverse, since they are collected only on the first $65,400 of pay in the United States and approximately the first Can$35,000 in Canada. Some 70 percent of American families pay more payroll than income tax, and payroll taxes alone push 1 million American children below the poverty line. Though the tax is ostensibly taken in almost equal parts from employers and employees, much of the employers' portion actually falls on employees in the form of lower wages.[26]

Environment: Payroll taxes raise the price of labor relative to resources, encouraging labor conservation rather than resource conservation.

Efficiency: Payroll taxes are fairly easy to administer.

Our grade: F   Your grade: _____

The Canadian finance minister announced the tax a day after his government announced plans to draft 100,000 men for service in the war, and the country accepted it as a matching "conscription of wealth." The personal income tax affected scarcely 1 percent of the population at first, but it later grew. In the meantime, the government introduced a corporate income tax and a manufacturer's sales tax, which, in the late 1980s, turned into a value-added tax called the goods and services tax. So it was that between 1910 and 1920, both the United States and Canada enacted all but one of their major modern taxes. (The lone exception is the payroll tax, which began with the U.S. Social Security Act of 1935 and a similar law in Canada in 1941.)[27]

At lower levels of government, the modern tax system was born mostly in the early 1930s, when many states reduced taxes on property by imposing taxes on personal and business income and on retail sales. For decades, Northwest states had relied on property levies for most revenues. (The province of British Columbia, a frequent exception, generated more money from public sales of natural resources than from the property tax until the 1920s.) In those days, property taxation was, in principle, wealth taxation. Levies applied to everything you owned, including not only real estate but also personal valuables such as jewelry and intangible assets such as cash, bank deposits, and stocks.[28]

In practice, however, the general property tax was a real estate tax. Tax agents lacked the power, now granted to income tax administrators, to require financial disclosures, so they could enforce the tax only on readily inspected assets such as real estate. This administrative failure meant that real estate owners, and especially farmers, paid

Property Taxes

The property tax, the foundation of local government finance throughout the Pacific Northwest, garners about one-quarter of state and local revenue in most Northwest states but less in British Columbia (see Appendix). The impacts of the property tax are split and contradictory because it functions as two different taxes: one on capital (such as buildings and machinery) and one on a natural resource (land). (For details, see "Sprawl Taxes.")

Economy: A tax on buildings engenders deadweight losses of roughly 24 cents per dollar collected. A tax on the value of land, because it is a tax on windfall profits, carries no deadweight losses and may even help the economy.[29]

Equity: A land-value tax is progressive: the wealthy own most land. A building tax is regressive: richer homeowners spend proportionately less on buildings than poorer homeowners, and building owners pass some of the tax on to tenants.[30]

Environment: A building tax encourages dispersed development and low-rise, car-dependent sprawl. A land-value tax encourages compact development, preserving open space.[31]

Ease of administration: Property taxes are immune to cheating, but administration is relatively expensive. The building tax is administratively more expensive than the land-value tax.[32]

Our grade: C (land-value, A; building, F) Your grade: _____

far more than their share. Uneven enforcement also ruined
public confidence in the tax; it was regarded as a sham.
Lesson 3. Easily evaded taxes lose the public trust. In
the 1920s, farmers began agitating for relief, offering the
state income tax as a cure for the shortcomings of general
property assessments.[33]

In Oregon, farmers and their trade union allies pushed
an income tax through the legislature in 1923, but a citizen initiative repealed the act months later. Four times
thereafter, voters rejected the income tax before the farm-
dominated legislature readopted it explicitly to reduce state
property taxes. Opponents again forced a referendum, but
the Great Depression had begun, and surging ranks of the
urban unemployed rallied behind the new tax on high
incomes. **Lesson 4. Keep trying.** Oregon expanded its
state income tax during the Depression, using it to completely offset funds from the old state property tax. Accustomed to the income tax, Oregonians have fiercely re-
sisted the sales tax, voting against it six times.[34]

In Washington, similar dynamics were in play, but—in
a classic example of the accidents that drive tax history—
they had the opposite results. The state legislature approved
an income tax in 1931, but the governor vetoed it. The
powerful farmers' Grange responded with an income tax
initiative that prevailed two to one at the polls. When the
state Supreme Court ruled the income tax unconstitutional, the Grange put a constitutional amendment before
the voters. But the political moment had passed. A state
property tax cap had won approval in the meantime, splin-
tering the income tax coalition, and the amendment went
down in flames. Shortly afterward, the state legislature

Sales Taxes

Sales tax rates range from zero in Oregon and Montana to 7 percent or more in Washington, California, and British Columbia (see Appendix). British Columbians also pay a federal goods and services tax, a value-added tax on each stage in the chain of production, which raises the effective sales tax rate to about 14 percent. Washington is the most reliant on the sales tax, depending on it for one-third of state and local revenue.

Economy: Deadweight losses come to 23 cents per dollar collected.[35]

Equity: Sales taxes exclude things that richer people buy disproportionately, such as private education, travel, second homes, land, and better medical care. The poorest fifth of households in Idaho and Washington pay three times as much of their income in sales taxes as do the richest fifth.[36]

Environment: Many goods with large environmental impacts—including electricity, heating fuel, gasoline, minerals, natural gas, pesticides, timber, and water—are exempt from sales tax in some or all of the Northwest.[37]

Ease of administration: Sales taxes are relatively simple to collect, except from mail-order sales.

Our grade: F   Your grade: _____

---

adopted a retail sales tax and a "business and occupations tax" on businesses' gross receipts—effectively a sales tax paid by the seller rather than the buyer. The sales and business

taxes, despite their heavy burden on those with low incomes and small profit margins, solved government's fiscal
woes. The system was no longer broken, so few saw reason
to fix it. Like Oregon in reverse, Washington grew accustomed to its taxes and rejected the income tax seven times.[38]

In California, too, Depression-era revulsion with property taxes led to a flurry of citizen tax initiatives. In 1933,
the legislature put its own proposal on the ballot, and voters decisively approved it. Called Riley-Stewart, the measure blew up California's existing tax regime and left the
legislature to create a new one. Sacramento immediately
adopted a retail sales tax, followed two years later by a state
income tax. By 1935, the bulwarks of California's modern
tax system were in place.[39]

In Idaho, meanwhile, Governor C. Ben Ross, a conservative but populist Democrat, won legislative approval of
the state personal and corporate income taxes long sup-
ported by farmers. In 1935, fearing the loss of federal relief
funds unless the state raised matching funds, Ross called a
special session of the legislature to institute a retail sales
tax. The levy—quickly dubbed "a penny for Benny"—did
not survive a subsequent referendum, but the state reen-
acted it in 1965 to eliminate state property taxes.[40]

The Northwest jurisdictions that did not construct their
modern tax regimes between 1910 and 1940 are British
Columbia and Alaska. B.C. created its income tax in 1876.
By 1910, when most places were just beginning to think
about modern taxes, B.C. also had a corporate income tax,
a variety of taxes on land and resources, and the usual general property tax. (The provincial sales tax came later, in
1948.) Alaska began to rely overwhelmingly on taxes and

Corporate Income Taxes

At the national level, only personal income and payroll taxes generate more revenue than corporate income taxes. Northwest states and provinces all depend on business taxes for about 8 percent of revenue. Instead of levying the usual corporate income tax, Washington taxes businesses' gross receipts.[41]

Economy: Corporate taxes discourage investment, penalize profit-making businesses, and badly distort business decisions. Deadweight losses from national corporate taxes alone are about 37 cents per dollar of revenue.[42]

Equity: Business taxes are superficially progressive, since rich individuals own most corporations. But because the taxes discourage enterprise, much of the cost is ultimately borne by workers, in the form of lost jobs and wages. Replacing corporate taxes with higher personal taxes for the wealthy would be better. Washington's tax falls heavily on start-up companies and others with small profit margins.[43]

Environment: Special tax rules favor mining, logging, and other high-impact activities. Washington's tax rate for service industries is three times the rate for manufacturers.[44]

Ease of administration: Most of the U.S. Internal Revenue Code is devoted to arcane rules about corporate accounting. This complexity raises compliance and enforcement costs.[45]

Our grade: F.   Your grade: _____

royalties from the oil industry with the opening of the trans-Alaska pipeline in 1977 and abolished its personal income tax three years later. One thing B.C. and Alaska did the same as other Northwest jurisdictions was to adopt taxes on motor fuels, cigarettes, and liquor in the 1920s and 1930s. Oregon invented the gas tax in 1919 and was quickly copied by its neighbors; most "sin" taxes began in the early 1930s.[46] **Lesson 5. Governments copy one another.**

Roll On, Complexity, Roll On

Drafted in the three decades before 1940, the list of taxes that revenue officers collect has since stayed remarkably stable. The rates have varied: national income tax rates have declined since World War II, while sales and payroll taxes have climbed substantially. But the tax burden has not shifted back onto property or trade. It has remained on income, profits, paychecks, and sales.

As important as changing rates has been the relentless accretion of special exceptions, especially in recent decades. Washington, for example, has enacted 222 of its 378 special tax giveaways since 1970. Oregon has enacted most of its 288 tax breaks in the past three decades. In both states, the value of tax exemptions actually exceeds the value of taxes collected; striking all exemptions would allow tax rates to be cut roughly in half. Instead, the piecemeal removal of more and more things from the base of each tax has pushed tax rates up. And rising rates have mobilized new interest groups to demand tax breaks of their own. This vicious circle of narrowing bases and rising rates added force, ultimately, to the tax revolts of the past two decades. These revolts—the fruits of years of organizing by business interests and property owners—have spread through the region in a wave of copycat lawmaking.[47] **Lesson 6. Political movements make all the difference.**

Like the tax revolts of the Great Depression, the more recent ones have centered on the property tax, probably because self-interested property owners form a huge voting bloc. California's Proposition 13 in 1978—imitated the same year in Idaho—reduced property taxes in the state by about $7 billion and locked in the reductions. If you owned a median-priced house, Proposition 13 was an opportunity to step inside the voting booth and write yourself a check for $870. (Interestingly, Proposition 13 won despite the overwhelming loss of three similar initiatives in the previous decade.) The following year, Washington voters capped the growth rate of their state government.[48]

Then, in the 1990s, Oregon voters twice capped or cut property taxes, doling out billions of dollars in tax savings to property owners as they approved measures that had lost at the polls as many as five times over previous decades. In 1993, Washington voters tightened the cap on the growth rate of state spending and also tied the legislature's hands by requiring that two-thirds of the members of both houses approve any tax increase or shift. A tax measure in Oregon had a similar effect, demanding supermajorities in the legislature and public votes for local tax and fee increases. As a result, Oregon voters find themselves studying mundane ballot proposals such as the 1997 measure to increase dog license fees by $2. In California, Proposition 13 and subsequent initiatives have also made voters, rather than legislators, the arbiters of many tax reform proposals.[49]

Flat-Tax Society

If the tax reforms of the early twentieth century shifted taxes off property and onto income, the trend of the late twentieth century has been to shift the burden from property and income onto payroll and sales. The tax burden has therefore moved from the rich onto the middle class and poor. In Washington, D.C., flat personal income taxes and national sales taxes are being seriously debated. At the state and provincial level, this trend is perhaps most visible in every jurisdiction's increased reliance on lotteries and other forms of gambling—revenue sources that are, though voluntary, nonetheless strongly regressive.[50]

No state in the Northwest has a tax system that is progressive or even truly flat, collecting an equal share of income from all classes. Worst of the bunch is Washington, which has the most regressive tax system in North America. The poorest 20 percent of Washington households spend three times as much of their income on state and local taxes as do the richest 20 percent. The middle 60 percent pay almost twice as large a share of their income as do the rich (see Figure 1).[51]

Some proposals for national tax reform center on taxing personal consumption rather than personal income. Taxing consumption is the right idea, but these proposals train their sights on the wrong kind of consumption. They would tax consumption as defined by orthodox economists: the sale of any good or service. What they ought to tax is consumption as defined by environmental economists: degrading the gifts of nature.

Still, recent developments in tax policy provide some hope for an environmental tax shift. Most jurisdictions have

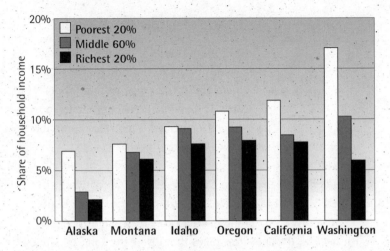

Figure 1. Who Pays What? State and Local Taxes, 1995
The poor pay a larger share of their income in taxes than the middle class—and the middle class pay more than the rich—in every Northwest state.
B.C. data unavailable. Sources: see note 51.

steadily increased taxes on health-threatening goods such as cigarettes and alcohol, earmarking some of the funds for medical care and health promotion. **Lesson 7. The current trend is toward flat taxes, consumption taxes, and "sin" taxes. Environmental taxes are all three.**

Many jurisdictions have also enacted small environmental fees, increased their reliance on user fees—such as infrastructure charges on developers and pay-by-the-bag trash collection charges—or trimmed subsidies for destructive activities. A green tax shift would build on this emerging trend. Your tax bill would reflect what you took from nature.

Taxes?! I Hate Taxes!

As they sit around the picnic table at their family reunion, the Joneses let off steam about their income and property taxes. If they had an accurate breakdown of their annual tax burden (see below), they would probably pay more attention to their sales and payroll taxes.

Even this tabulation is not complete, because it doesn't include hidden taxes that the Joneses pay indirectly. The Joneses' payroll tax burdens, for example, effectively double because of the matching payroll taxes their employers pay. These and other business taxes that lower the Joneses' wages and limit their job opportunities escape notice even more than the sales and payroll taxes they pay directly.

Idaho Jones downs his Budweiser—the bestselling beer in America—and fumes over his property taxes. Little does he know that taxes made up about 43 percent of what he paid for the can in his hand.[52]

The Joneses' Taxes

	B.C.	Idaho	Ore.	Wash.
Household income	Can$55,000	$40,500	$46,200	$49,600
State, provincial, and local taxes				
Sales and excise taxes	957	1,701	323	3,770
Property taxes	1,380	729	1,594	1,389
Income taxes	4,086	1,256	2,379	0
Federal taxes				
Payroll taxes	2,920	3,098	3,534	3,794
Income taxes	6,508	3,851	4,706	5,216
Value-added tax (GST)	1,135	0	0	0
Total	**Can$16,986**	**$10,635**	**$12,537**	**$14,169**

Sources: see note 53.

WHAT WE
COULD HAVE

Taxes could reinforce—rather than contradict—our shared beliefs in the importance of individual freedom matched with individual responsibility, of work and personal initiative, and of fairness. They could strengthen our economy and improve our environment. And they could do so equitably and with greater ease of administration than the existing system. In short, we *can* get taxes off our backs and onto our side.

Furthermore, we could design a tax shift that matched revenue sources with the appropriate level of government. That way, local problems such as traffic jams would be answered with local taxes; state and provincial problems such as air pollution would be addressed with state and provincial taxes; and global problems such as climate change would be remedied with national taxes.

Carbon Taxes

Slowing global climate change is among the largest environmental challenges facing the world, and it is disproportionately a North American problem. North Americans emit more than twice the quantity of climate-threatening greenhouse gases per person as do Western Europeans,

roughly four times the global average. The consequences
of climate change are likely to be severe in the Northwest,
including worsened floods, droughts, and forest fires.[54]

One good way to reduce North American emissions
is to impose a carbon tax—a tax on fuels in proportion to
the carbon dioxide they emit—and parallel taxes on other
greenhouse gases. These taxes would raise the prices of
gasoline, electricity from coal, and other goods with big
climate impacts. But the rise would be gradual and pre-
dictable, allowing everyone from homeowners to major
corporations to adapt. People would switch to more effi-
cient vehicles, equipment, and appliances and do more er-
rands on foot, on bike, and on-line. More passengers and
freight would move by rail rather than by air. More home
buyers would ask about energy bills, consider energy-
saving apartments and condominiums, and look for residences closer to work. In billions of individual choices, the
interests of the climate would become a consideration, not
through conscious do-goodery but through the persua-
siveness of the price tag.[55]

Revenues from carbon taxes could finance reductions
in payroll taxes. Shifting from regressive, antilabor payroll
taxes to carbon taxes would be a mild tonic for employment growth and a strong tonic for wage growth. It would
provide for seniors' retirement while safeguarding the climate in which they will retire.[56]

A tax of $100 per ton of carbon, with parallel rates on
other greenhouse gases, would have raised $5.8 billion in
the Northwest in 1994, assuming a 15 percent reduction
in emissions. It would offset more than one-fourth of all
payroll taxes collected in the region and save the typical

working household $852 a year. A tax of this magnitude
would add 27 cents to the price of a gallon of gasoline
(Can$0.11 per liter), increase the wholesale price of natu-
ral gas by 50 percent, and raise the price of coal by 180 percent. It would also reduce greenhouse gas emissions.
Although we would pay more for gasoline and heating,
the lower payroll taxes would leave most working northwesterners with more money in their pockets.[57]

Shifting from payroll taxes to carbon taxes would reduce
the regressivity of the tax system, with one notable exception. Low-income retirees and other nonworking poor
households do not pay payroll taxes, but they would pay
carbon taxes. Partial rebates or other means of compensating these households would address this hardship.

The service sector would benefit greatly from this tax
shift. The biggest losers would be the Northwest's handful
of coal-burning power plants and ten aluminum smelters,
which together account for one-tenth of the region's greenhouse gas emissions. Some plants might close; others would
convert to cleaner fuels or more-efficient industrial processes. Displaced workers might need transitional aid, but a
gradual tax shift would allow the economy to absorb them.
And the pain of carbon taxes would be nothing compared
with the pain of full-fledged climate change.[58]

Ideally, climate protection taxes would be national levies
paired with matching carbon tariffs on imports, to prevent
an influx of foreign goods manufactured in polluting plants.
But states and provinces could encourage national action
with starter taxes at modest rates. In the Northwest, state
and provincial taxes of just $10 per ton of carbon would
have yielded $578 million in 1994.[59]

Pollution Taxes

Not counting greenhouse gases, more than 3.5 billion pounds of harmful pollutants flow into the Northwest's environment each year. Though simply adding up tons of different pollutants is a bit like adding apples and oranges, the sheer volume of it all is staggering. No less thought-provoking is the total of overtly dangerous substances: more than 4 million pounds of toxic materials entombed in landfills; 39 million pounds dumped into rivers and lakes; and 63 million pounds dispersing, like a puff of smoke, into the air we breathe.[60]

Even seemingly harmless pollutants can have sobering consequences. The primary cause of poor water quality in Washington and Idaho is not the discharge of toxins from manufacturing plants but the runoff of manure and other fertilizers from farms. Small particles suspended in the air—by-products of burning wood, coal, and motor fuels—pose grave dangers to our lungs.[61]

Other threats arise from the 250 or so human-made chemicals that reside in the fatty tissues of almost every living person in North America. This chemical contamination is a prime suspect in the rising rates of reproductive disorders, including life-threatening tubal pregnancies and endometriosis, an often painful, fertility-impairing condition that afflicts about 5.5 million North American women. Among males, average sperm counts have fallen 50 percent since World War II.[62]

Cancer is also increasingly common. It now strikes more than one in three and kills about one in four North Americans; men are at greater risk than women, and Americans are at greater risk than Canadians. U.S. cancer rates climbed

54 percent from 1950 to 1994; rates have also increased in Canada, but somewhat more slowly. In both countries, the prevalence of breast and prostate cancers, already high, is growing fast. Childhood cancer, once a rarity, has also become all too common: if present trends continue, one of every 400 American children born this year will contract leukemia, brain cancer, or some other cancer before his or her fifteenth birthday. Surging cancer rates cannot be explained entirely by aging of the population, changes in smoking rates, hereditary factors, or better detection techniques.[63]

Suspicions about the role played by the vast quantities of toxic chemicals in our air, food, and water are difficult to prove. Cancer may result from the cumulative effects of multiple exposures to various combinations of the 75,000 or so synthetic compounds in wide commercial use. Five to 10 percent are estimated to cause cancer, but fewer than 3 percent have been definitively tested one way or the other. Nonetheless, researchers have shown that cancer death rates are higher in U.S. counties with hazardous waste incinerators and other major environmental contaminants and that exposure to solvents and pesticides at home or at work can endanger not only adults but their children as well. Other studies have revealed or suggested links between "hormone mimics"—chemicals that our bodies mistake for human sex hormones such as estrogen—and breast and prostate cancers and other reproductive system maladies.[64]

North American environmental protection agencies have banned some of the worst human-made chemicals, but their overarching failure to protect public health is unsurprising given the Herculean scope of their task and the limitations of regulations. Regulations must, by their

very nature, take a continuum of risk and divide it in two:
allowed (i.e., "safe") and not allowed (i.e., "unsafe"). Nine
parts per million of the insecticide malathion on a Washington apple is considered an unacceptable risk to public
health, but eight parts per million is considered harmless.
Because regulations allow for no middle ground, a host of
factors—including the entrenchment of chemicals in our
economy, well-financed political opposition, and scientific
uncertainties—have all but forced regulators to err not on
the side of caution but on the side of the status quo, giving
the green light to a vast assortment of questionable chemicals and activities. And because regulations cannot acknowl-
edge the existence of a continuum of risk, they are unable
to provide incentives for manufacturers and others to ex-
plore or invest in safer alternatives.[65]

Regulations are the best way to control the most dangerous chemicals, but taxes can help address the vast gray
areas along the continuum of risk. Taxes can take into account what we know about different chemicals—their tox-
icity and persistence, for example—with higher tax rates
for more dangerous substances. Just as important, taxes can
take into account what we don't know about different
chemicals. Scientific suspicion that a certain chemical con-
tributes to cancer, for instance, might not be enough to
justify banning that chemical, but it could easily justify an
increased tax rate. The tax could even incorporate a "sur-
charge on uncertainty" that would rise over time, giving
companies an ever-stronger incentive to conduct safety
tests or switch to previously tested materials. Pollution taxes
would smooth a transition out of our current dependence
on tens of thousands of risky substances.

Point sources The most obvious targets of pollution taxes are factories, sewage treatment plants, and other facilities where pollutants come out of pipes or smokestacks. Pollution taxes in use in North America and around the world highlight their ability to provide cost-effective pollution control. In the Netherlands, a hefty charge for dumping lead, mercury, and other heavy metals into rivers is the main reason that water pollution levels dropped more than 90 percent between 1975 and 1995. As part of the phase-out of ozone-depleting chlorofluorocarbons (CFCs) in the early 1990s, the U.S. government imposed taxes that raised CFC prices as much as 11-fold, spurring innovations that quickly produced low-cost alternatives. Tradable emissions permits, which are related to taxes, have helped the U.S. Environmental Protection Agency (EPA) control the sulfur dioxide emissions contributing to acid rain. Germany and France have made headway with water pollution charges, as have Wisconsin and New Jersey.[66]

Current environmental regulations provide ready-made tools for taxing point sources. Managers of point sources must already monitor and report their emissions of many pollutants, and most governments in the Northwest already levy small fees based on these reports. Pollution taxes could use this administrative framework to generate revenue without new bureaucracy.[67]

Pollution taxes consist of two components: a relative tax rate, which weighs the dangers of different chemicals against one another, and a baseline rate, which applies to the "average" chemical. For example, if the baseline rate were $2 per pound and arsenic were ranked as 50 times more dangerous than average, then the tax rate for arsenic

Permit Me to Pollute

If pollution can be taxed like cigarettes or any other commodity, what makes it different from any other commodity? Well, nothing, really—a point made explicit in tradable permit systems such as the U.S. Environmental Protection Agency's five-year-old sulfur dioxide (SO_2) program. Every year, EPA issues a limited number of "permits to pollute," each of which gives its owner the right to emit one ton of SO_2. Companies can then buy or sell these permits like so many shares of stock or sacks of potatoes. By reducing the number of permits issued each year, EPA will reduce SO_2 emissions in the year 2000 to half their 1980 levels.[68]

Tradable permit systems are more complicated than pollution taxes, in part because governments must hold an annual auction to generate revenue from permits. Pollution permits and taxes are closely related, however, in that both use economic tools to make polluting expensive. The details of reducing pollution are left to the invisible hand of the free market. Economic incentives aim to achieve low-cost pollution reduction and to stimulate innovation by giving businesses and inventors an opportunity to make a profit (or cut costs) by reducing pollution. The SO_2 permit program is a case in point: entrepreneurial and technological advances have cut the cost of reducing SO_2 emissions from $660 per ton in 1992 to about $100 in 1997.[69]

Despite its successes, the commodification of pollution has troubled some observers, who question the morality of buying and selling the right to pollute. Still, the alternative to selling permission to pollute is, in practice, to give away such permission for free, a policy unlikely to reduce emissions and more likely to increase costs for all involved.

would be $100 per pound. Setting relative rates is an imperfect science, but existing air and water quality standards, together with point-source emissions limits, provide an introductory system that's in place now for weighing the impact of different pollutants. In Wisconsin, for example, severe limitations on discharge levels identify the most dangerous water pollutants, which are taxed at higher rates than pollutants with fewer discharge restrictions. Modifications to such off-the-shelf systems can accommodate special needs in different localities.[70]

The ideal tax rate, according to economists, charges polluters for the costs they impose on others. These "external" costs include environmental damage, health impacts, and economic losses. Finding this optimal tax rate is easier said than done, but scholarly estimates of the human and environmental costs of pollution suggest that the optimal rates are many times higher than the fees in place now. The fee for emitting a ton of sulfur dioxide, for instance, is about $50 in most regions of the Northwest, but the costs of that pollution—including crop losses, building and monument corrosion, impaired visibility, and respiratory illnesses—may be $5,000 or more. Gradually increasing pollution taxes until they approximate the true costs of polluting would add economic teeth to the regulatory approach of pollution control agencies. Had they been in place in 1995, pollution taxes would have raised $3.1 billion in the Northwest, assuming a 15 percent reduction in emissions. (See Appendix for detailed pollution tax rates and revenues.)[71]

Shifting current business taxes (mostly corporate income taxes) onto pollution would not greatly affect the

overall level of business taxes in the Northwest, but the tax
rates for specific companies and industries might change
substantially. With big polluters bearing more of the tax
burden, small entrepreneurs—the source of two out of every three new jobs in America—would get a break. The
growing service industry and other "clean" sectors would
also benefit handsomely. And increased demand for pollution reduction programs would further strengthen the
Northwest's green technology sector.[72]

While "clean" companies would benefit, "dirty" companies would pay for the messes they make. One analysis
of the impact of water pollution charges in Washington
State found that more than half the taxes would be levied
against polluters in one industry: pulp and paper manufacturing. It's easy to see why: inventories of major toxic polluters in Oregon and Washington read like a *Who's Who* of
the pulp and paper industry. And while British Columbia's
government was the first in the world to establish a dead-
line—the year 2002—for the elimination of dioxins and
other deadly by-products of chlorine bleaching, its coun-
terparts in the United States have dragged their feet, despite a call by the nation's largest public health association
for a phaseout of industrial chlorine use.[73]

Other major polluters would also be held responsible
for their wastes. Sewer systems would be improved in
municipalities like Vancouver, B.C.—where the Annacis
Island plant regularly shows up on B.C.'s list of the province's
worst polluters—and Seattle, where 2.2 billion gallons of
raw sewage was dumped into the waters of Puget Sound
in 1996. Coal-burning power plants, like the one in
Centralia, Washington, whose sulfur emissions are estimated

to kill more than 19 people each year, would have to clean up their act. So would coal and metal mines, which rival pulp and paper mills as polluters. And pollution taxes would not pass over huge chicken-, hog-, and cattle-raising "factory farms," which environmental agencies consider point sources of pollution.[74]

Even though pollution charges could be increased gradually to give companies time to adopt new technologies and production processes, hefty pollution taxes nonetheless seem to pose a threat to the viability of manufacturing businesses, especially if foreign competitors do not face similar standards. Yet research by Harvard Business School professor Michael Porter reveals that pollution taxes and other environmental protection measures have the same effect as the emergence of rival firms: existing businesses may not like them, but the innovations they inspire create stronger, more competitive companies. Indeed, numerous case studies involving firms such as Boeing, Ford, and the Canadian telecommunications company Nortel highlight environmentally inspired changes in production processes that resulted in less pollution, higher-quality products, lower costs, and greater employment.[75]

Pollution taxes would encourage manufacturers to stop investing in—and dumping—vast quantities of chemicals and to start investing in the people and innovations that offer low-cost pollution solutions. And should these solutions prove too costly, companies would end up paying the pollution tax and raising the prices of their products. A properly designed pollution tax would therefore make prices tell the truth about the environmental damage done during manufacturing.

Farming: Beside the point? Although factories and
other point sources are still a huge environmental problem, small or scattered nonpoint sources, most notably
motor vehicles and farms, have steadily gained in notori-
ety. Fertilizer runoff—which stimulates algal blooms, de-
pletes oxygen, and threatens fish populations—damages tens
of thousands of miles of rivers and streams in the Northwest, including one-third of those in Washington State. By
the 1980s, pesticides had contaminated groundwater supplies in about one-fourth of counties in the American part
of the Northwest. With agricultural chemical use and cancer deaths linked in nearly 1,500 rural U.S. counties, pesticide trade names like Revenge, Max-Kill, and Hel-Fire
take on new meaning.[76]

To crop producers, agricultural chemicals have major
benefits: a dollar invested in pesticides, for example, returns
about $4 in crops saved. But that dollar also results in at least
$2 in off-the-books damage to the environment.[77]

Regulations have for the most part failed to deal with
these dangers. Controls on fertilizers are so minimal that
some U.S. fertilizer manufacturers legally mix hazardous
wastes into their products. Pesticide regulation has an
equally dismal record. A 1993 study by the National Acad-
emy of Sciences concluded that, despite 30 years of effort
by EPA to evaluate pesticide safety, lack of information
made it impossible to determine if pesticide regulations
adequately protected children. Other studies suggest that
pesticide regulations leave farmworkers at much greater
risk of occupational injury and illness than others.[78]

Where regulations fail, taxes can succeed. Thanks in
part to a 30 percent sales tax on pesticides, Sweden—where

farmers' use of pesticides roughly matched that in Oregon or Montana—reduced pesticide use by almost 50 percent between 1985 and 1990. Using tax revenue to fund research and education programs can help farmers adjust and bring substantial additional reductions in pesticide use.[79]

Fertilizer taxes can be easily piggybacked on existing programs in which Northwest governments partly finance fertilizer inspection programs by imposing a tax of a few pennies per ton. Pesticides would be more difficult to tax, in part because only California carefully tracks their sale or use. Like a tax on industrial emissions, pesticide taxes could use a ranking system—such as the one developed by the Environmental Health Policy Program at the University of California, Berkeley—to differentiate between compounds, imposing the highest taxes on compounds that pose the greatest danger to people and the environment. Hefty tax rates might be needed to achieve significant reductions in chemical use, but even moderate tax rates would stimulate farmers, researchers, and governments to devote more attention to low-chemical cultivation.[80]

Fertilizers and pesticides each make up about 4 percent of farm production costs, so even doubling their prices would raise farm costs by at most 8 percent. But farmers would likely discover ample opportunities to trim chemical use, softening the tax blow. In the Netherlands, which provides about 65 percent of the world's exported cut flowers, actions taken to reduce environmental harms have lowered costs and improved product quality. Cornell professor David Pimentel argues that pesticide use on major Northwest crops such as apples and potatoes could be reduced by 50 percent with little or no increased cost to the

Tax Evader #1: Farms

Farms are among the worst of-
fenders in water pollution, toxic
chemical use, and habitat destruc-
tion, but they get special favors under existing tax
laws. In Washington, for example, farmers and food processors got $268 million in sales and business tax breaks in 1997,
including sales tax exemptions on fertilizers and pesticides.[81]

Property tax breaks are also huge: $122 million a year in
Oregon and Washington. Those handouts stem from the belief
that agriculture is dominated by family farmers who, in the
face of soaring property tax bills, would have no choice but to
sell to developers. To prevent this scenario, Northwest governments tax farmlands at their "current use" value—the value of
farmland as farmland rather than as a potential housing
development—which gives farmers tax discounts of up to 95
percent. Yet most farms are not threatened by urbanization at
all: some 84 percent of Oregon farmland assessed at use value
is in eastern Oregon, far from large cities. And farmers who do
face pressure can trim their taxes with conservation ease-
ments. For most landowners, though, the joys of farming do
not hold a candle to the big money offered by developers. The
research literature on farm taxation is unequivocal: use-value
assessment does not slow sprawl.[82]

A tragic irony of use-value assessment is that "hobby farmers" seeking tax breaks have swept into farmlands. Thousands
of suburban dwellers in Ada County, Idaho, plant alfalfa to
reap property tax deductions of up to 95 percent. In the
Fraser River valley around Vancouver, B.C., hobby farms, golf
courses, and developers have taken over much land suppos-
edly reserved for agriculture.[83]

farmer and that a 50 percent reduction in pesticide use in the United States as a whole could be achieved with only a 1.5 percent increase in consumer prices.[84]

A pesticide tax averaging $8 per pound, roughly double the current average cost of pesticides, would account for the $2 in external costs that arise from each $1 spent on pesticides. The costs of fertilizer use are difficult to quantify, but a tax of $75 per ton would tack roughly 50 percent onto the price of fertilizers. Together, these taxes would have generated $700 million annually in recent years, assuming a 15 percent reduction in use.[85]

Such a tax shift would bring tremendous benefits to the Northwest. Consumers would have fewer worries about pesticides at the dinner table. Retail food prices would increase only slightly, if at all. Less chemical runoff would greatly improve water quality for drinking, recreation, and wildlife. The greatest beneficiaries of such taxes, though, might be agricultural communities in the Northwest, especially if the revenue were used to offset current taxes that damage farm economies. Higher chemical prices would make knowledge-intensive farms more competitive relative to chemical-intensive farms, encouraging farmers to adopt low-chemical alternatives like integrated pest management. Farm jobs would be safer, and wider use of techniques such as scouting and forecasting could raise employment levels. As chemical use declined, dollars previously captured by the agrochemical industry would recirculate within rural communities, boosting the economy. And taxes on agricultural chemicals would reverse the perverse incentives that lead farmers to poison themselves, their families, and their surroundings in order to survive.

Driving: A particular problem Just as damages from nonpoint sources of water pollution have surpassed those from point sources, the harms from nonpoint sources of air pollution—such as woodstoves, solvent use, and motor vehicles—are outpacing those from smokestacks. The most serious threats to air quality in the Northwest are tiny inhalable particles (also called fine particulate matter) that can worsen respiratory diseases, especially for children and the elderly. Researchers in Seattle estimate that inhalable particles are responsible for 12 percent of emergency room visits for asthma. In addition to missed days of school and work, inhalable particles can result in hospitalization and even death. Analysis of two long-term studies by Harvard Medical School and the American Cancer Society suggests that particulate pollution kills more than 1,800 northwesterners each year.[86]

The main sources of the most dangerous inhalable particles (those smaller than 2.5 microns in diameter, about 28 times thinner than a human hair) are not natural sources like windblown dust but human activities. Particulate pollution results directly from fuel combustion in woodstoves, coal power plants, and motor vehicles, and indirectly from atmospheric reactions involving other dangerous air pollutants such as ozone and sulfuric acid. The worst polluters are the 11 million cars, trucks, and buses that crowd our roadways and garages. Collectively, they are responsible for about half the air pollution emissions in the Northwest's major metropolitan areas.[87]

The most commonly discussed market-based solution to our car troubles is the gas tax, either by itself or as part of a carbon tax intended to combat global warming. But

Tax Evader #2:
The Car

Existing tax laws give cars the green light at every turn. In British Columbia and Washington, the tax breaks start before cars even roll out of the dealership: buyers can subtract the value of any used car they trade in from the price of the new car they are buying before calculating sales tax. This handout cost Washington governments $120 million in 1997.[88]

B.C., Idaho, and Washington exempt motor fuels from retail sales taxes; in Washington, this giveaway was worth $214 million in 1997. They and other Northwest jurisdictions impose gas taxes but earmark the proceeds for roadwork, so governments' general funds do not benefit. Even in Alaska and British Columbia, the only parts of the Northwest that do not earmark gas tax receipts, road spending usually exceeds fuel tax revenue. California applies both fuel taxes and sales taxes to gasoline but still earmarks the entire revenue stream for roadwork. Local jurisdictions in Washington, Oregon, and Idaho, meanwhile, spent almost $500 million from property and other general taxes on roadwork in 1993. As a result, the true tax rate on gasoline—factoring in roadwork subsidies—is negative.[89]

Finally, parking—whose provision costs substantially more than the fuel northwesterners put in their tanks—gets off lightly under existing tax codes. Most parking in the Northwest is given away for free and is untaxed. The U.S. federal income tax exempts the value of employee parking, a $3-billion-a-year handout nationwide. Canada in effect does the same thing. In both countries, subsidies to drivers who are affluent are larger than to transit riders who are poor.[90]

while emissions of carbon dioxide are proportional to the amount of fuel a vehicle consumes, emissions of urban air pollutants depend heavily on other factors such as the age and condition of the vehicle and the type of fuel used. As a result, increasing gas taxes is not the only—or even the best—way to improve urban air quality.[91]

A superior strategy would be to charge drivers for the estimated costs of their vehicles' emissions. During the regular emissions inspections that already take place in all of the Northwest's major metropolitan areas, each vehicle's per-mile emissions would be measured, and odometer readings would reveal the number of miles driven that year. Multiplying the two figures yields an estimate of the car's yearly emissions, for which the driver would have to pay according to the same tax rates that apply to point sources. Such a tax—averaging $135 per car—would generate $1.5 billion in revenue (assuming a 15 percent reduction in emissions) and give a powerful boost to the development and use of cleaner vehicles.[92]

Mileage-based emissions fees would be especially helpful for diesel-powered vehicles, which can emit 30 to 100 times more inhalable particles than comparable gasoline-powered ones. Phased in slowly, such a policy would be the best tool for improving air quality. But several first steps could set the stage. Higher gas taxes or per-mile insurance charges could lessen gasoline consumption. (See NEW's *The Car and the City* for more ways to reduce our driving.) Other tax shifts could improve air quality by changing our driving habits and our choices of cars and fuels.[93]

For instance, over 80 percent of the pollution from a typical five-mile urban drive comes during the first minute, when the engine is too cold for the pollution-cutting cata-lytic converter to work properly. These "cold start" emis-sions would diminish if trips were combined or eliminated; land-value taxes (discussed later in this chapter) could help by encouraging more compact development. Additional gains in air quality could come from reducing traffic con-gestion, since stop-and-go driving generates emissions three to four times higher than normal.[94]

Another option is to promote cleaner fuels, which are held back by seemingly insignificant price differences. Reformulated (or oxygenated) gasoline cuts emissions by 15 percent but is hard to find in the Northwest because it costs five cents more per gallon than regular gasoline. California's tough standards for diesel fuel, which reduce emissions of inhalable particles by up to 25 percent, raise diesel prices by only about six cents per gallon—also not much, but enough to effectively banish "California diesel" from most of the Northwest. Governments can make clean fuels competitive by shifting the burden of fuel taxes from clean fuels to dirty ones. Tacking a five- or ten-cent sur-charge onto the most polluting fuels and giving a similar discount to the cleanest fuels would promote cleaner fuels without affecting the majority of gasoline purchases.[95]

Even greater gains, in both the short and the long term, could come from cleaning up cars. Some 20 percent of the vehicles currently on the road are responsible for as much as 80 percent of automobile emissions. Simply repairing or replacing these superpolluters—mostly old or malfunction-ing vehicles—would cut on-road emissions by about three-quarters. One possibility is to exempt the best-performing 20 percent of vehicles from existing annual license and registration fees and double the fee on the worst-performing 20 percent of vehicles. Such a "20/20" tax shift, while leaving the middle 60 percent of vehicles completely unaffected, would give a few drivers an annual bonus for investing in clean vehicles and other drivers a pricey reminder that their wheels are behind the times. This type of policy would be easy to implement in localities throughout the Northwest that already require emissions tests.[96]

A longer-term strategy to encourage the development and purchase of cleaner vehicles would be to change the tax rates on new cars. Again, a "20/20" program, with the worst-performing new cars paying all or some of the taxes for the best-performing ones, would reap tremendous benefits without affecting the majority of new car buyers. California's legislature passed a similar proposal in 1989, but the governor vetoed it. Even a tax shift of $100 per car might work wonders: that sum represents the price difference between a standard vehicle and a low-emission vehicle that pollutes only 30 percent as much. The importance of a seemingly trivial few hundred dollars was highlighted in early 1998 when Chrysler's president hesitated to adopt design changes that would reduce pollution from sport utility vehicles by 40 percent, because such changes would add $200 to its Jeep Grand Cherokee's $30,000 sticker price.[97]

A final option is to involve businesses in the search for low-cost pollution reduction strategies. Once point-source pollution taxes are in place, hard-hit businesses could qualify for tax credits by fixing or buying out superpolluters, installing vapor recovery systems in gas stations, or taking other measures to improve urban air quality. Each ton of emissions such a program eliminated would offset some of

the business's own emissions and thus reduce its tax bill.
Some regions in California run similar "cash for clunkers"
programs.[98]

Traffic Taxes

Survey after survey finds that people consider traffic congestion the worst problem in the metropolitan Northwest.
Hardly surprising. Seattle has the sixth-worst gridlock in
the United States, and Portland, at fourteenth worst, is not
much better. Congestion in these two metropolitan areas
wastes 130 million hours of residents' time and 143 million gallons of gasoline each year. The situation in
Vancouver, B.C., is also dismal.[99]

Motorists enraged at government ineptness, population growth, or one another may find small comfort in the
axiom of transportation planning first enunciated by economist Anthony Downs in 1962: traffic volumes will inevitably overwhelm urban freeways during peak hours. Congestion happens, Downs warned, adding that it would be
futile to convert our cities into "giant cement slabs."[100]

Thirty-five years later, many northwesterners still in-
stinctively cling to the idea of expanding our 220,000-
mile highway network. But this supply-side strategy is
finally losing its sheen. Overshadowing air quality concerns and neighborhood opposition is fiscal necessity. In a
time of constrained budgets, citizens and elected officials
are hesitant to spend billions for more pavement. In Portland, a gas tax increase of $1.25 per gallon would be needed
to fund the estimated 60 miles' worth of new highway
lanes required each year to mount a serious assault on congestion. With bridge expenses driving road-building costs

above $10 million per mile, planners in Seattle and Vancouver, B.C., face similar financial constraints.[101]

As road building's stranglehold on the Northwest's transportation imagination loosens, citizens and their elected officials are shifting their focus from increasing the supply of asphalt to reducing the demand for it. Under the rubric of "transportation demand management," officials are looking at everything from promoting and enhancing transit service, bicycling, carpooling, and telecommuting to limiting parking, raising gas prices, and turning freeways into tollways. Having thrown our pocketbooks at the problem for 30 years, we are now throwing the kitchen sink as well.

Unfortunately, we are moving too slowly, and not always in the right direction. Present transportation plans will continue to make heavy demands on the public purse over the next 20 years. In Seattle and Portland, the costs of the planners' preferred systems exceed anticipated revenues by billion of dollars and, if fully funded, would still hardly dent the gridlock that awaits us down the road.[102]

Even if the Seattle area digs up almost $1 billion extra each year to spend on mass transit and other transportation improvements, afternoon gridlock will spread to almost half the freeway network in the central Puget Sound region by the year 2020. The time residents spend stuck in traffic will grow threefold over 1995 levels; average highway speeds will fall to 21 miles per hour. Ditto for Portland: even if voters approve an extra $4.7 billion in road-building projects, drivers inside the urban growth boundary can expect to spend twice as much time in traffic jams by 2015. Ditto again for Vancouver, B.C., where rush hours will tie up 60 percent more vehicles in 2021 than in 1992.[103]

In this extended-rush-hour gridlock, commuters will find themselves vying for space with parents driving their kids to school, retirees on social outings, and teenagers on shopping trips. By giving everybody equal and unlimited access to a valuable commodity, government policy has created inefficiencies that rival the breadlines of communist Russia. Those breadlines hint at a solution—quite possibly the only solution—to traffic jams: charging for the use of busy roads. Providing a scarce resource for free, be it a loaf of bread or highway space at rush hour, inevitably leads to gridlock. Seven years after the fall of the Soviet Union, it may be time for North America to give the free market a road test.

The Northwest could attack congestion and revenue needs simultaneously by imposing tolls (to be collected at full speed using "smart cards" and modern electronics) on busy roadways during busy hours; the toll would rise as rush hours approach and taper off as traffic dwindles. Such a system, known as congestion pricing, has the potential to transform northwesterners' transportation decisions. Some travelers—truckers, for example—will pay the fee and reap the benefits of less congested roads. Some will take the bus or join a carpool. Others will minimize their costs by adopting innovations like telecommuting or "casual carpooling." Still others will decide to postpone their trip to the mall until rush hour is over or to walk to a neighborhood store instead. Everyone using the roadway will have an incentive to economize his or her use of a valuable resource, and everyone—on the road and off—will benefit from the hundreds of millions of dollars in tax breaks funded by toll revenue.[104]

The People's Transit

Few activities bring out the ingenuity of North Americans like avoiding taxes. With congestion pricing, this inclination would be harnessed to reduce gridlock. Around San Francisco, tolls and gridlock have resulted in "casual carpooling," in which drivers cruise by suburban transit stops and pick up commuters. Passengers save on bus fare and get a quick ride downtown. Drivers get to speed along in the carpool lanes and don't have to pay tolls. Used daily by about 10,000 commuters in the Bay Area, casual carpools have also formed in Washington, D.C.[105]

Truly an organized coincidence, casual carpooling develops spontaneously. Its emergence and growth depend not on government policy but on favorable conditions, including tolls, carpool lanes, and other incentives for would-be drivers to leave their cars at home and for will-be drivers to pick them up. A reliable transit service is also vital, both as a backup and to provide easily identifiable pickup locations.

As congestion worsens and budgets tighten, more areas are examining congestion pricing. Vancouver, B.C.'s transportation plans assume that the city will stem the flood of cars into downtown by imposing $2 tolls on Burrard Peninsula bridges; Portland is considering implementing a congestion-pricing pilot program. It may not be long before the Northwest takes a hint from Orange County in southern California, where drivers have to pay to use the express lanes that a private company added to Route 91.

As congestion pricing becomes more familiar both in the Northwest and elsewhere, drivers may calm their fears and hesitantly embrace the advantages of toll roads.[106]

Two concerns are that tolls would slow traffic and intrude on drivers' privacy. Fortunately, "phantom tollbooth" technology would allow drivers to pay tolls without slowing down and without compromising their privacy. Instead of stopping at tollbooths, drivers would place prepaid toll cards—purchased at gas stations—in their windows. Scanners along the roadway would deduct tolls as cars pass. The system would be completely anonymous as long as drivers possessed the toll cards; scofflaws, travelers, and others without toll cards would have their license plates photographed for later billing. Similar systems are already in place in southern California and around the world.[107]

Another concern is that tolls would impose a heavy burden on the poor. Studies suggesting that congestion pricing is likely to benefit the rich more than the poor seem to confirm the regressive nature of tolls. But there are three extenuating circumstances. First, using toll revenues to reduce bus fares or expand bus service would make congestion pricing substantially more progressive. Second, congestion pricing focuses both the costs and the benefits of tolls on rush-hour commuters. The large benefits for the wealthy come not just because they have no problem shelling out a few bucks to speed things along, but also because they tend to spend a lot of time on the road during peak hours. Lower-income individuals who would have more difficulty paying the tolls are less likely to be on the roads during peak hours and so are well situated to avoid paying the tolls at all. Third, worsening

gridlock benefits no one. Lost time, wasted gas, and higher
transportation costs harm everyone, both rich and poor.
The rich may benefit the most from congestion pricing,
but almost everyone will end up with more time on their
hands, more money in their pockets, or both.[108]

Analysis of the Seattle area highlights the crucial role
that congestion pricing is likely to play in any viable transportation solution. If nothing is done to solve the region's
transportation problems, planners at the Puget Sound Regional Council (PSRC) predict that afternoon commuters
in the year 2020 will waste over four times as many hours
in traffic backups as they did in 1995. Implementing congestion pricing plus a kitchen sink of other tactics would
result in what PSRC calls the "optimum performance strategy": 2020 afternoon commute delays only 26 percent
above 1995 levels. Congestion pricing is the linchpin of
this strategy. Without it, the "kitchen sink" scenario by itself will lead to a 3.4-fold increase in afternoon delays—
and $21 billion in unpaid transportation bills.[109]

Nonetheless, PSRC decided only to continue studying congestion pricing. The obstacle was not technical but
political. In an age of resentment over government intru-
sion and waste, proposals to tax roads are unpopular.

Ironically, this resentment of big government may in
the end speed the adoption of tolls. The big-government
programs that built our national highway systems are coun-
terproductive now that our biggest transportation problem is congestion. Matching funds from higher levels of
government reward suburbs with disastrous land-use planning, distract local decision makers from low-cost alternatives, and expend vast sums to briefly delay gridlock.

The current trend toward devolution—handing powers and duties down to lower levels of government—could bring us back to our senses. Higher government levels could get out of the transportation business entirely by handing over control of gas taxes and gas tax revenues, along with responsibility for maintaining and expanding road and transit systems, to city and county authorities. As metropolitan residents, businesses, and governments realize that they are on their own—that help is not on the way—they will face their steadily worsening gridlock with enhanced interest in low-cost transportation solutions.

With or without devolution, congestion pricing is bound to get attention. Opponents are sure to resist, for free ways die hard. But governments can take baby steps without provoking drivers' ire by sponsoring demonstration projects, such as the one under consideration in Portland. And, should congestion pricing remain beyond the pale, voters and their elected officials will have only two choices: they can do nothing and watch the problem get much worse, or they can spend a lot of money and watch the problem get much worse.

Sprawl Taxes

The mirror image of suburban sprawl is urban decay: boarded-up buildings, vacant lots, and derelict neighborhoods. In every Northwest city, there is ample room for development around urban centers, in close-in neighborhoods, and in underused commercial and industrial zones. And filling in our cities is the only way to avoid filling up our countryside. It is also the only way to create cities in which automobiles are not king. Most Northwest jurisdictions seek to prevent sprawl through the regulatory tools of land-use planning; none applies taxes to the same task. Yet a simple reform to the existing property tax would turn it into a powerful incentive for investment in city and town centers and in adjacent neighborhoods.

A property tax is actually two conflicting taxes rolled into one. It is a tax on the value of buildings and a tax on the value of the land under those buildings. As experience in Australia, New Zealand, Taiwan, and Pennsylvania shows, shifting the tax from the former to the latter aids compact development while suppressing land speculation, promoting productive investment, and tempering housing costs, especially for the poor. It does these things because of the unique nature of land values.[110]

In land values, location counts for everything. Land in a crime-infested, rundown neighborhood is worth a fraction as much as an identical lot in a safe, popular neighborhood. Paradoxically, though property owners can increase their building values by improving their buildings, nothing they do to the property will change their land values. Only their neighbors, government, and society at large can do that. Government actions are especially important, and they usually increase land values. If a city builds a park, a province expands transportation infrastructure, or a nation restores a historic landmark near a parcel, the land's value will rise. Government-caused reductions of land values are called "takings," but "givings" through acts like these are in fact more common.[111]

Location matters a great deal to people. In King County, Washington, which includes Seattle, the assessed value of real property was $107 billion in 1993. Of that, only $61

Tax Evader #3: Mansions

Big houses are a big environmental issue. As much as 40
percent of the raw materials consumed in North America go
into constructing, maintaining, and heating buildings. Tax
policy encourages us to live in big houses on big lots—
speeding sprawl—and to invest in second homes, which are
often built on fragile slopes and shorelines.[112]

Federal income tax deductions for mortgage interest,
property taxes, and homeowners' capital gains (earnings
from rising land values) totaled $80 billion nationwide in
the United States in 1997, and nearly half the benefit went
to households with annual incomes above $100,000. The
U.S. government gives more housing assistance to families
with six-figure incomes than to the poor.[113]

State income taxes, most of which are coupled to the
federal tax, increase the value and inequality of these handouts. Oregon lost $383 million to homeowner tax breaks in
1996. They cost Montana $50 million in 1997, of which 84
percent went to the richest 30 percent of households.[114]

Canada's tax breaks for housing are smaller and better
focused. Neither mortgage interest nor property taxes are
deductible, although capital gains are lightly taxed.
Homeowners do get an income tax credit for property taxes
paid, but the credit helps mostly the poor and middle class.
As a result, about the same proportion of Canadians own
their homes as Americans, but Canadians live in smaller
residences.[115]

billion represented the value of private buildings—approximately what it would cost to reconstruct them. The re-
maining $46 billion came from the value of land—what
people would be willing to pay purely for location. In Vancouver, B.C., the assessed value of land in 1994 was Can$51
billion, while buildings were worth Can$19 billion.[116]

And location matters more as time goes by. As incomes
rise, people spend an increasing share of their earnings on
location. Historically, urban land values have increased faster
than population, the consumer price index, or income. The
real value of private land in King County multiplied nine-
fold from 1976 to 1995. In economic terms, rising wealth
is capitalized in land values; in common parlance, to quote
comedian Will Rogers, "Buy land, because they ain't makin'
any more of it." In the 1990s, prices for homes in all the
Northwest's major cities have skyrocketed, climbing 9 percent annually in King County and even faster in metropolitan Portland. The run-up in housing prices is due to
fast-growing populations with fast-rising wealth competing for the same parcels of urban space.[117]

Because land is a rare commodity whose worth increases through actions of everyone except the owner, land
speculation is possible. Most successful investments, whether
in businesses or buildings, create salable products not oth-
erwise available. The investor makes money, and consumers have more of what they want. But successful land speculation—buying land to hold it until its value increases—fails
the public. It does not create any salable good or service; it
prevents full use of premium sites, shunting development
to less desirable locations. The investor makes money, and
society has less of what its members want.[118]

Take a tour of any Northwest city, and, if you look for them, you will notice that a surprising share of private lots hold rundown buildings or no buildings at all. In Seattle, such a tour could begin immediately across the street from the city's venerable Pike Place Market, where—on land worth more than $100 per square foot—almost an entire block is full of parking lots and derelict buildings. One houses a strip joint. One, an eight-story building, has been vacant above the second floor since 1975. Much of the block is part of the empire assembled by land speculator Sam Israel, who accumulated 40 parcels in downtown Seattle and dozens of others elsewhere. After Israel's death in 1994, the *Seattle Times* noted, "He owned more property in downtown Seattle—and had done less with it—than any other private landowner in the city."[119]

Typical buildings on fully used downtown lots are worth three to four times as much as the land under them. Israel's decrepit downtown buildings, taken together, were worth half as much as the land under them. Holding his 5.4 acres of prime urban sites out of full development meant pushing thousands of offices, apartments, and shops out of the urban core. And Israel, whose properties are at last being developed by his successors, was unusual only in the scale of his business and in its eventual exposure to public scrutiny. A study of eight randomly selected urban and suburban neighborhoods in King County found that between 8 and 63 percent of land is vacant or dramatically underdeveloped. In the city of Seattle, land zoned for residential development could hold an additional 113,000 units of housing. All development in fast-growing Clark County, Washington—a suburb of Portland—would fit easily into two-thirds the land area if developers filled contiguous sites before leapfrogging to remote ones. And building compact, walkable neighborhoods rather than sprawling subdivisions would shrink the footprint of development in the county to one-third its actual size.[120]

Land speculation is parasitic, not productive. Its antidote is to shift the property tax off buildings and onto land. Exempting buildings from the property tax and shifting its full burden onto land values would have put Sam Israel out of business—or into the business of developing premium sites rather than hoarding them. It would have boosted his Seattle tax bill by $200,000 a year, eliminating almost all the profits he might have hoped for from land-value appreciation. To pay the tax, he would have had to generate more income by developing or selling some of his parcels.[121]

Shifting property taxes from buildings onto land increases development of the most valuable sites, especially in city centers, but also in suburban centers and other already developed areas. Parking lots—a standard holding pattern for land speculators—give way to buildings. Density increases. Supplies of apartment and office space increase. Rental prices moderate.

Modeling results for King and Clark Counties, Washington, show that land-value taxation would more than double taxes on parking lots and vacant building lots, increase taxes by up to one-quarter on car-oriented commercial strip development, and moderately reduce taxes on pedestrian-oriented neighborhood shopping districts. It would reduce taxes by about one-third on the most land-efficient forms of housing—apartments and condo-

WHAT WE COULD HAVE

miniums—and by about 5 percent for single-family residences. In King County, taxes would rise slightly for single-
family homeowners in the most central neighborhoods,
encouraging creation of accessory, or "mother-in-law,"
apartments; in Clark County, industrial facilities would save
more than one-third of their tax bills.[122]

In both counties, these changes are averages that mask
wide ranges of outcomes. Under land-value taxation, the
tax burden shifts in proportion to the intensity of land use
on each property; it makes no difference whether that parcel
is urban or suburban, expensive or cheap, commercial or
residential. The question is whether the site is used to its
potential. If it is, the tax burden will decrease; if it is not,
the tax burden will increase. (Indeed, one weakness of land-
value taxes is that they encourage development not only
in urban areas but also along fragile shorelines and other
popular scenic areas. Land-value taxes are good at con-
taining sprawl; other policies are needed to protect eco-
logically important areas.)

Finally, shifting the property tax onto land is highly
progressive because land ownership is concentrated in the
hands of the affluent. Indeed, the distribution of land ownership is much more skewed than the distribution of income. Those who own no land benefit enormously, and
even most middle-class homeowners benefit, because their
houses are usually worth more than their land.[123]

Exempting all buildings, equipment, and other capital
from the property tax, and making up the lost revenue
through higher rates on land values, would yield the same
revenues for localities, states, and provinces in the Pacific
Northwest as they currently garner from property taxes—

some $11 billion in 1996. But it would turbocharge existing growth management plans, encouraging full development in urban and suburban centers, along with more compact development elsewhere in cities.

You Must Pay the Rent

The concept of economic rent is central to understanding land-value and resource taxation. Rent is windfall profit, profit that accrues to a company not as a result of its skill and hard work, but because it succeeds in gaining private control of a public good of exceptional value. Urban land values are a clear example of economic rents: they reveal the worth of a location, not the worth of what a landowner has built at that location. Normal profits benefit society by attracting competitors to a market, ultimately lowering prices for consumers and reducing profits for producers. Where profits result from economic rents, however, competitors cannot enter the market because the owner has locked up the resource. Taxing away windfalls from owning prime urban real estate, therefore, does not raise the price of urban sites; it only reduces the profits.[124]

Windfalls sometimes also accrue to owners of mineral rights, timber concessions, commercial fishing permits, water rights, and dam licenses. Taxing away these rents does not affect prices either; it yields public revenue without any deadweight losses. But because rent taxes leave prices unchanged, they do not usually encourage resource conservation. Land-value taxes succeed in that goal only because they prevent land speculation.

Raising land-value taxes still higher—to collect more revenue than current property taxes generate—would neither impose deadweight losses on the economy nor penalize the poor. And it would only increase the tax's benefits against sprawl and sky-high housing prices. In this book, though, we are arguing only for a shift of the property tax onto land values. If funds were ever needed to cover revenue shortfalls, land-value taxes offer a better recourse than conventional taxes on income and capital.

Resource Consumption Taxes

The environmental impacts of the human economy are especially pronounced at the economy's feeding end—the industries that extract energy, timber, water, and other natural resources. Lump these industries together and you have the league leaders in habitat destruction and species endangerment. You also have the providers of raw materials that pass through the human economy, where the industries that process, transform, transport, and dispose of them generate another large share of environmental harm. Taxing extraction tells everyone to conserve natural resources, encouraging recycling, efficiency, and frugality from the sawmill to the shopping mall to the garbage dump.[125]

States and provinces can levy taxes to reflect environmental harm; they can also tax resource rents—windfall profits from resource extraction. These latter taxes offer no immediate environmental benefit because they do not change prices, but they are strongly progressive and could generate hundreds of millions of dollars in additional funds without causing deadweight losses. Besides, capturing windfalls often requires no new tax; instead, it requires charging

market rates for public resources. The public, after all, owns
most timber stands and mineral deposits in the Pacific
Northwest—which is 75 percent public land—along with
all wild fish, hydropower sites, and fresh water. Yet governments give away many of these resources for free or sell
them at fire-sale prices.[126]

Existing taxes on resource rents and resource consumption—on fish, fossil fuels, hydropower, minerals, timber, and
water—generated $2.3 billion in 1996 in the Northwest.
Some $1.8 billion of that total accrued to British Colum-
bia, where resource taxes and royalties account for 13 percent of local and provincial revenue.[127]

Water Taxing diversions of water from lakes and rivers,
and its extraction from underground aquifers, would stem
the enormous inefficiency in water use in the Northwest,
safeguard fish and aquatic habitats, and increase hydropower
production by leaving more water in streams. Among
Northwest jurisdictions, only B.C. charges fees for with-
drawing water from the public realm, and it charges as
little as one-sixth of a cent per thousand gallons. (Elsewhere, people pay for water delivery, not for the water
itself.) In the rest of the Northwest, a tax of $20 per acre-
foot—$0.06 per 1,000 gallons—would have generated more
than $600 million in 1995, assuming a 15 percent reduc-
tion in consumption induced by higher water prices. In
Idaho alone, which consumes more water per person than
any country in the world, it would have yielded $288 mil-
lion, offsetting half the state's sales tax.[128]

A tax of that size would be too small to notice for anyone but irrigators, who use 81 percent of the water pumped

or diverted in the Northwest. Phasing in the tax over a decade would soften the blow, allowing farmers to improve their equipment and adjust their cropping patterns. Administering the tax would be simple. Much water delivered to farms is already measured; where it is not, monitoring is neither difficult nor expensive. Alternatively, states could tax irrigators' water rights, which would encourage them to shed unneeded rights and speed the water-rights adjudication proceedings grinding on in many Northwest basins.[129]

A tax of six cents per 1,000 gallons would have only a slight effect on food prices. In California, even if the entire tax were passed on to consumers, it would raise the price of a hamburger with all the fixings by about four cents, the price of a pound of flour by two cents, and the price of a pound of fresh tomatoes by less than one-fifth of a cent. It would add five one-hundredths of a cent to the price of an order of french fries from Idaho. In an age of surging populations and endangered salmon, a gallon of water is surely worth at least six one-thousandths of a cent.[130]

Hydropower What water remains in Northwest rivers flows through dozens of large hydroelectric dams—dams that generate power at a price about 40 percent lower than the continental average. But just as fossil fuels' environmental impacts go unmentioned in market prices, hydropower actually costs more than its price. To reflect the cost of decimated salmon runs and other consequences, state and provincial governments could, as Idaho does, tax hydropower and use the proceeds to offset other taxes. A one-half cent per kilowatt-hour environmental tax on hydropower would have generated $1.1 billion in 1996.[131]

Meanwhile, another kind of tax on hydropower could turn the advancing deregulation of the North American electricity market—which threatens to spread low-cost Northwest power to other regions even while stranding Northwest ratepayers with old debts such as that from the Washington Public Power Supply System debacle—into a

Tax Evader #4: Energy

Energy consumption is favored with plentiful tax exemptions.
The federal governments of the United States and Canada go easy on the energy industry, mostly through special accounting rules. In the United States, federal tax breaks of about $2 billion went to oil, coal, alcohol fuel, and other energy industries in 1997. Because most states and provinces base their income taxes on federal rules, they lose additional revenue to these provisions. Montana lost half a million dollars a year in 1992 and 1993.[132]

All Northwest state and provincial governments except Alaska exempt from the general sales tax not only motor fuels, but also electricity, natural gas, and some other fuels, though in B.C. the exemption applies only to residential consumers. A patchwork of other taxes, including utility receipts taxes and kilowatt-hour taxes, make up some of the difference, but these taxes are small and irregular. Idaho, for example, imposes a slim tax on electric power—but only if it is hydropower; only if it is generated in the state; and only if the consumer isn't using it for irrigation, mining, minerals processing, or manufacturing.[133]

major tax shift opportunity. At present, the choices about deregulation seem limited to bad (cheap power but no wild salmon) and worse (neither cheap power nor wild salmon). But there is a third, little-mentioned possibility: governments could embrace deregulation and—through taxes on private dams and treasury contributions from public dams—claim any windfall profits that deregulation brought the region's dam operators. A small share of the resulting revenues could pay for salmon protection and energy conservation programs, which utilities find difficult to support in a competitive market.

Turbines in Northwest dams produce one-third of North America's hydropower, and the Northwest's big dams are among the least expensive electricity generators in the nation, so in the end, the Northwest may come to use its power efficiently at home and sell the surplus. The profits could help fund the region's governments, much as taxes on windfalls from oil and gas extraction generate two-thirds of Alaska's revenue. B.C.'s tax on windfall profits from natural gas production demonstrates how a hydropower rent tax might work: the tax rate is minuscule when gas prices are low but rises in step with prices. For hydropower, such a price-dependent tax might ultimately result in revenues of one cent per kilowatt-hour, once deregulation is complete. Had deregulation and a hydropower windfalls tax been fully phased in by 1996, the tax would have generated $2.2 billion for Northwest governments.[134]

Timber The price of timber does not include the environmental costs of logging, such as lost wildlife habitat, erosion into mountain streams, and worsened floods from logged-over watersheds. A tax of $20 per thousand board feet of timber, perhaps collected by the same administrators who gather existing timber taxes, would have generated $565 million in the Northwest in 1992 and tilted the wood products market toward recycled materials.[135]

Northwest governments could retrofit existing timber taxes into true environmental levies. Oregon could simply raise its tax of $4 per thousand board feet. British Columbia already imposes a tax on logging, but Ottawa effectively assumes this tax burden by counting every dollar a company puts toward the logging tax against the company's federal income tax bill. Canada could end that exemption. All Northwest states and provinces but Oregon already collect modest timber harvest taxes in lieu of property taxes on standing private timber. (Oregon collects timber harvest taxes in lieu of property taxes on private timber*land,* not on the timber itself.) All the jurisdictions could separate the harvest tax from the property tax, making it clear that there is no tax on growing trees, only on cutting them down. They could also extend the harvest tax, as does Washington, to public as well as private timber.[136]

To capture windfalls from public timber, governments could sell permission to log public timber only when the sale is above cost and at market prices, and only when it passes environmental review. British Columbia, which owns more Northwest forest than anyone else, sold trees at a small fraction of their value until the early 1990s, when the province raised prices substantially, dedicating most of the proceeds to a new program of forest restoration and economic development in timber towns. The higher prices brought in an extra Can$452 million in 1996; an open

Tax Evader #5: Timberlands

Private timberland owners, who hold the most productive wood-growing land in the region, enjoy many of the same property tax breaks as farmers, with the same unintended consequences. Montana taxes timberland at one-sixth the average property tax rate in the state. Every other state and province in the Northwest taxes timberland, like farmland, at current-use values.[137]

Because lighter taxes apply to timberland than to natural forests—in British Columbia, the tax burden is reduced by half or more—the main physical impact of use-value taxation is to encourage logging on fragile land. The main fiscal impact is to reduce government revenue: $31 million a year lost in Oregon, $4 million a year in Washington, and millions more elsewhere.[138]

These regional handouts come on top of federal giveaways such as the bizarre accounting loophole called "expensing of timber-growing costs" that delivers $200 million nationwide annually to U.S. timber owners. States that piggyback their income taxes on the federal code lose millions more: $12 million in Oregon, for example, and $3 million in Montana.[139]

auction of logging permits probably would have generated still more. The U.S. Forest Service, the region's second-largest landowner, auctions off most of its timber concessions but accepts bids far below the full cost of building associated roads and selling the timber. In 1996, national forests in the Pacific Northwest (including southeastern Alaska, northwestern California, and western Montana) lost $156 million on timber sales.[140]

Fish Commercial fishing in Washington and Oregon is almost defunct after a century of habitat destruction and overfishing, but to the north the industry remains stronger. Existing taxes on fishing in the Northwest—commercial fishing taxes, sport fishing licenses, and commercial fishing permits—help stem overfishing and also help pay for fisheries programs. They yielded $156 million in 1996 in the Northwest, including Alaska. But they do not capture all the rent. If they did, fishing licenses would not trade for exorbitant prices, as they do in northern British Columbia, where a commercial fishing license can garner Can$120,000. Revising these taxes to capture resource windfalls might double the revenue.[141]

Minerals One of the most environmentally damaging industries, mining is a shadow of its former self in the Northwest. But since the 1980s, miners have learned to use solvents to extract metals from mountains of crushed rock, and proposals for new mines are sprouting up across the region's map. Where these controversial projects can pass environmental review, states could tax them to capture windfalls, perhaps doubling revenue. (Only B.C. now generates more than token revenues from mines.) Reforming the 1872 Mining Act could ensure that the U.S. government received the windfalls from mines on federal lands.[142]

Environmental taxes on virgin minerals would reflect environmental costs while encouraging conservation and recycling. Taxing minerals at a percentage of sale price would roughly approximate environmental impacts, because an ore's value determines how much land the miners can afford to disrupt in its pursuit. A 10 percent tax on virgin nonfuel minerals extracted in the Northwest states would have yielded $127 million in 1995.[143]

Other public assets that governments could tax without distorting the economy include the broadcast spectrum, whose use is distributed mostly by application rather than by auction, and airspace for landings and takeoffs from airports. Air travel is polluting, noisy, and energy intensive.

What Environmental Taxes Cannot Do

Taxes are powerful tools, but there are many jobs they cannot do. The biggest limitation of tax mechanisms is that there must be something to tax. This simple fact can be problematic in cases where it's impossible to measure the damage one wants to tax—for instance, soil erosion, overgrazing, and other bad land-stewardship practices—or where measuring the problem is expensive or intrusive, such as pollution from woodstoves, lawn mowers, and barbecue grills. Taxes also cannot clean up existing messes, such as the Hanford Nuclear Reservation, the Superfund mining sites in the Rockies, the salmon-killing design of many dams, or the half-million miles of logging roads lacing Northwest forests. In these cases and others—such as protecting coasts and other scenic and important zones from development—regulations and other strategies are necessary.

Together, taxes on natural resource rents would power economic development by removing deadweight burdens from the economy, while taxes on resource consumption would steer the economy toward conservation and efficiency. Though rent taxes would be progressive, consumption taxes would be regressive, requiring compensating reductions in other regressive taxes or rebates for the poor. Water and electricity consumption, logging, mining, and fishing would all decline somewhat. But everyone would gain from the overall effects: closer alignment between the means of public finance and public ends.

Adding It Up

Combining local congestion and land-value taxes; state and provincial pollution, land-value, and resource taxes; and national greenhouse gas taxes—all at the rates described in this book—would have yielded $29 billion in 1996, enough to offset 28 percent of all tax revenue collected in the Northwest. Counting existing fuel taxes, sin taxes, and other revenue sources that do not penalize work or investment, 39 percent of all government revenue collected in the region would have come from taxes on bads rather than goods.[144]

At the federal level, taxes on greenhouse gases would have generated $5.8 billion from the Northwest, one-third of it in B.C. These environmental taxes could have replaced 60 percent of payroll taxes in British Columbia, and as much as 25 percent of payroll taxes in the Northwest states.[145]

In states and provinces, pollution, traffic, resource, and land-value taxes levied at the rates described in this book for the year 1996—assuming 15 percent reductions in pollution and water use—would have yielded $24 billion. Existing fuel taxes, sin taxes, and other revenues that did not penalize work and investment actually generated $10 billion. Thus, of a total of $40 billion of revenues collected that year, green taxes could have readily generated all but $6 billion (see Figure 2 and Appendix).

The tax package described in this book would produce different results in different parts of the region. In British Columbia, for example, had the tax shift been fully phased in by 1996, it (along with existing revenue sources that did not fall on labor or capital) would have generated 82 percent of B.C.'s provincial and local revenue. In B.C., pollution and hydropower taxes would have yielded the most new revenue, aside from the reformed property tax on land values. Overall, such a tax shift would have eliminated all property taxes on buildings (as everywhere in the region), plus almost all provincial corporate income, sales, and personal income taxes.

In Idaho, the same tax package would have supplied 85 percent of the state's revenue, offsetting three-fourths of all state corporate income, personal income, and retail sales taxes. Water-use taxes would have been the largest new source of revenue. This tax shift would have displaced 70 percent of Oregon's taxes on labor and capital, allowing the state to eliminate corporate income taxes and exempt poor and middle-class households from personal income taxes. Pollution and hydropower taxes would have been the twin leaders among new revenue sources. Washington's hydropower taxes would have yielded the most new revenue in that state under a tax shift. Overall, the state would have bid farewell to two-thirds of its taxes on labor and capital. It

Actual

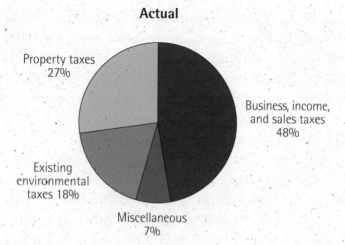

Property taxes
27%

Business, income,
and sales taxes
48%

Existing
environmental
taxes 18%

Miscellaneous
7%

Tax Shift Scenario

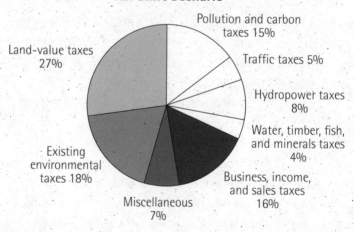

Pollution and carbon
taxes 15%

Land-value taxes
27%

Traffic taxes 5%

Hydropower taxes
8%

Water, timber, fish,
and minerals taxes
4%

Existing
environmental
taxes 18%

Business, income,
and sales taxes
16%

Miscellaneous
7%

Figure 2. Sources of State, Provincial, and Local Revenue, Pacific Northwest, 1996
Taxing "bads" at rates that reflect environmental costs would largely fund governments.
Sources: see Appendix.

could have scrapped the business and occupations tax and lowered the sales tax rate by more than half (see Appendix).

Of course, these calculations are all illustrations, not conclusive revenue projections. A real-world Northwest tax shift would be unlikely to end up with the specific tax rates assumed here. Indeed, it would probably begin very small; the largest environmental tax shift in the world to date, in Denmark, changed the source of only 2.5 percent of revenue. The important point is that taxing bads at rates that reflect environmental costs would largely fund local, provincial, and state governments. As a practical matter, however, tax reforms come in pieces, not wholes, so perfecting the grand design of a tax shift would be largely academic. More salient is to assess the strengths and weaknesses of the rough-hewn new taxes already described.[146]

Economy The beauty of tax shifting is that it promotes public goals, such as environmental protection, even while it spurs the economy by removing deadweight—the stifling impacts of taxes on work, savings, investment, retail spending, and building. Taxes on resource rents or windfalls carry no deadweight losses. Pollution taxes and other taxes that improve the environment create some deadweight losses—for example, by discouraging enterprise in polluting industries. But because taxes on environmental harm reduce environmental costs in the economy—such as health-care costs for people sickened by pollution—these losses tend to be much smaller than those from taxes on labor or capital. Other new taxes might even lead to net economic gains by eliminating economically damaging activities. Land-value taxes push funds invested in unproductive speculation into productive investments. Traffic taxes minimize the time, money, and resources squandered in gridlock. Overall, the tax shift we describe would have increased economic output by at least $5 billion, or 1.6 percent.[147]

Equity The impact of a tax shift on different income groups depends on the details. Land-value taxes, resource windfall taxes, and pollution taxes on businesses are progressive; that is, the tax burden rises with ability to pay. Carbon, hydropower, motor vehicle pollution, and resource consumption taxes—because they raise the prices of consumer goods—are either proportional or regressive. (Rebates for the poor would help: everyone would pay the full price of high-impact goods and services, but governments would distribute the average tax liability, perhaps $500 per person, to qualifying low-income families.) Reducing sales and payroll taxes would improve the fairness of the Northwest's tax systems, and a tax shift would further help equity by spurring the economy, boosting the supply of affordable housing, and increasing wages.

Environment A tax shift would save hundreds, perhaps thousands, of lives each year by improving air and water quality, stemming traffic, and curtailing the use of toxic substances. (Raising cigarette and alcohol taxes would save additional lives.) The environment would benefit too. Pollution taxes would clean up our air, water, and land. Water taxes would help protect rivers and the salmon and other wildlife that depend on them. Traffic and land-value taxes would reduce auto-related pollution and resource consumption and protect rural lands by braking sprawl. Carbon

"Tax Shift?"
"After You."

Would everybody have to shift taxes at the same time? In a global economy, how can a handful of states and provinces, or even two countries, impose heavy taxes on pollution and resource consumption without simply putting themselves at a competitive disadvantage?

In a tax shift, a few scurrilous polluters would probably relocate or shut down, but for all but a few industries, taxes on labor and capital hurt competitiveness much more than do taxes on pollution and resource consumption. The Northwest's biggest exporters, by value, spend much more on brainpower than on raw materials, and would therefore benefit from lower taxes on labor. Furthermore, traffic taxes and land-value taxes would help competitiveness by speeding commerce and lowering the price of rented building space.[148]

In fact, the first jurisdictions to shift taxes—far from getting pummeled for it—might reap the largest economic rewards. Getting taxes out of the way of work and enterprise could turn early shifters into magnets for clean, nimble companies at the vanguard of the economy.

taxes would slow global warming, with all its attendant human and environmental harm. And resource taxes would dampen the economy's appetite for resources extracted from forests, mines, and rivers, taking pressure off natural ecosystems. Exactly how much our environment would benefit depends on the strength of the pollution taxes and how

clever people turn out to be at preventing pollution and
conserving resources.

Administrative ease Some new taxes—such as electronic
road tolls, pesticide taxes, and taxes on pumped groundwater—would require new collection mechanisms, but most
could piggyback on existing procedures. Pollution tax collection could buttress existing pollution reporting and fee
requirements. Water taxes could rest on top of irrigation
districts' existing water delivery charges. Electricity taxes
and carbon taxes could come in tandem with existing fuel
and utility taxes. To carry the load of tax collection, existing administrative procedures would require improvements—better staffing, fuller enforcement—but few brand-

Think Globally, Shift Locally

Local jurisdictions have relatively few choices in
tax policy, but that need not stop them from
implementing tax shifts of their own. By law,
Alaskan towns can include gasoline in their sales tax; Montana counties can tax both gasoline and natural resources
such as coal; Washington cities can tax parking lots; and Oregon and Washington counties can, with voter approval, put
slim taxes on gasoline. Since Washington law is ambiguous
about how cities can tax businesses, localities could tax businesses based on their pollution emissions, their solid waste
bill, or their number of parking spaces. Throughout the region, localities can experiment with traffic tolls, as Portland is
hoping to do with federal support.[149]

new bureaus. And taxpayers would find environmental taxes simpler to comply with than corporate and personal income taxes.

Transition A tax shift could phase in new taxes gradually over several years, giving everyone time to adjust. A gradual transition would be especially important for the most vulnerable communities. Towns that depend heavily on the most-polluting facilities, industries that cater to the automobile, logging towns, and communities that benefit from subsidized irrigation water would see their overall tax loads increase. But the simultaneous reductions in payroll, sales, income, and business taxes, and in property taxes on buildings, would provide some relief. And during the phase-in, everyone could aggressively pursue lower-impact practices.

Another reason for a gradual phase-in is to guarantee governments the revenue they need. Pollution and resource consumption taxes are unfamiliar tools of public finance; no one yet knows how much pollution and resource consumption they will wring out of the economy. If people turn out to be exceptionally good at greening their lives and businesses, revenue from pollution and resource consumption taxes will decline somewhat. But traffic congestion charges and taxes on land values are likely to generate growing revenue streams. A phase-in would give governments time to fine-tune the tax system.

A phase-in would also give reformers time to guard against a potential weakness of environmental taxes: they can send strange incentives to government agencies, and even to citizens. The U.S. Forest Service and many Northwest counties have traditionally favored timber extraction over other uses of forestlands, probably because both the agency and the counties get to keep some timber sale proceeds, unlike other Forest Service revenues. Alaska's reliance on royalties from the oil industry has made the state and its citizens receptive to new oil extraction proposals. On the other hand, such strange incentives are not ubiquitous. High tobacco and alcohol taxes do not seem to sway government bodies to support smoking or drinking. Still, the problem merits scrutiny.[150]

Tax Shifting with the Joneses

How would a tax shift affect the Joneses? Though it's tempting to claim that they would all be better off—after all, they are average northwesterners, and tax shifts will, on average, help more than they hurt—the truth is that it depends. It depends on where they live. Shifting property taxes onto land values will benefit apartment dwellers more than owners of spacious urban lots. Offsetting payroll or sales taxes with carbon taxes will benefit urban dwellers like Oregon and Washington more than rural resident Idaho, who logs more miles in his Ford F-150 pickup (the most popular wheels in his state) than his siblings do in their Honda Accords (the most popular in their states). It depends on where they work. Shifting business and payroll taxes onto pollution may hurt the manufacturing sector, but it will help the service sector, which employs most of the Joneses. It depends on how they spend their time and their money. The Joneses, whether or not they commute regularly, will have to weigh the costs and benefits of using tolls to reduce gridlock. And above all, it depends on their ability and willingness to change. The Joneses who can best adapt to new taxes—for instance, by purchasing energy-efficient appliances, trading in a sport utility vehicle for a compact car, renting out an unused bedroom in their house, or carpooling instead of solo commuting—will gain the most financially from a tax shift.[151]

HOW TO GET IT

The Boston Tea Party started a North American tradi-
tion: the tax revolt. Rural rebellion against tariffs in the
Populist era set in motion the reform process that led to the
personal and corporate income taxes, which arguably made
possible this century's growth in national, provincial, and
state governments. A few decades later, homeowners rebel-
ling against rising property taxes limited the growth of state
and local governments. People from many walks of life may
lead the next tax revolt: a shift of taxes from "goods" to
"bads." Such reform could gather as much support from
corporate boardrooms as from union halls, from public
housing projects as from tree-lined streets, from environmental activists as from champions of small business.

Tax shifts pursue liberal ends, such as ecological restoration and a living wage, by conservative means, such as
relying on free markets and rewarding enterprise. Tax shifts
pursue conservative ends, such as personal freedom and
responsibility, by liberal means, such as making the pol-
luter pay. Instead of the usual political or class divisions, tax
shift politics are likely to divide people in unfamiliar ways,
pitting service-sector businesses against resource industries,
low-mileage drivers against high-mileage drivers, conspicu-

ous recyclers against conspicuous consumers, and developers against speculators.

In some parts of the Northwest—British Columbia, in particular—elected leaders may carry forward the tax shift revolt. If they do, they will certainly make the most popular changes first: perhaps shifting a portion of business taxes onto major point-source polluters or lowering sales tax rates by extending the base to include pesticides. They may experiment with land-value taxes in areas zoned for commercial uses or in depressed neighborhoods desperate for new development. Unless public finances explode into crisis, elected tax shifters will proceed cautiously and incrementally, and they will take steps to lower the political costs of tax shifting. They may put in grandfather clauses for older property owners or caps on tax increases for favored industries.

In other parts of the Northwest, especially in the American states, tax shifts may bypass elected representatives through citizen initiatives. In Oregon and Washington, supermajority requirements for legislative tax proposals virtually guarantee that tax reform will have to come from popular votes on ballot measures. Polling-place tax shifts are likely to be as piecemeal as legislative ones because complicated ballot measures rarely win voter approval. And major tax reforms in the histories of almost all the Northwest states have involved initiative campaigns that succeeded only after several attempts.

What could stop a tax revolt that makes so much sense? Those who profit most from the existing tax system will no doubt try to stop it. These include, in the short term, land speculators, resource extractors and processors, and

Strategies for Tax Shifters

Tax reform, whether it comes from legislative halls or voting booths, is rarely pretty. German chancellor Otto von Bismarck said that the two things you don't want to watch being made are laws and sausages. Here's some advice for sausage makers.[152]

1. **Plant seeds everywhere.** Every level of government has opportunities to shift some portion of the tax burden off labor and capital and onto the gifts of nature. Waiting for a national shift may be less valuable than demonstrating the concept in counties, cities, states, and provinces. As history reveals, tax reform can be contagious: tax-writing committees often copy one another.

2. **Organize your allies.** Try to build a coalition out of the disparate forces—including businesses, labor unions, political organizations, communities, and taxpayers—that lose big from the existing system and can win big from tax shifts.

3. **Don't write anyone off.** Heavily polluting industries, for instance, might support taxes that target all polluters (including nonpoint polluters such as drivers and farmers) as a way to level the playing field. (Regulations tend to target factories and other point sources.) Within the high-impact industries, furthermore, interests are not monolithic. The cleanest and nimblest companies in polluting sectors of the economy may anticipate being able to beat the competition at keeping costs down, thus gaining an advantage.

4. **Remember that all tax dollars are not the same.** Economists may think that a dollar's a dollar, but everyone else seems to play favorites. Try to shift the burden onto taxes that are relatively popular (such as taxes paid by businesses and that "other people" will pay) and off the taxes that people hate most.

5. **Keep trying.** Oregonians approved the personal income tax on its sixth try. Property tax caps like California's Proposition 13 have usually won only after several failed attempts. Some new taxes may face legal barriers. The courts might reject land-value taxes in Washington State because of ambiguous provisions in the state constitution. But the high-profile lawsuit leading up to the decision would stimulate public education and debate, building momentum for constitutional change.

6. **Think big.** The tax system is so unpopular that fundamental reform is not unthinkable. The bigger the shift, the more people will save.

7. **Start small.** The tax system is so powerful that even little changes—such as the "20/20" tax shifts for reducing motor vehicle pollution—can have large repercussions.

8. **Say "Shift, shift, shift."** Many people will suspect that a tax shift is really a tax increase in disguise. Be sure to separate the issue of *what* government taxes from the issue of *how much* it taxes.

Idaho Jones and the Tax Crusade

Nothing unites the Joneses like a common enemy, and taxes are a frequent target of their anger. But knowing that roads, parks, police, and schools must be paid for somehow, they love to hate some taxes and merely hate others. Business and other taxes that they don't pay directly escape their wrath. Sales and payroll taxes also go little noticed, their hefty tallies lost in a flurry of receipts and pay stubs. Tax shifters targeting these taxes would do well to engage the Joneses in dialogue about the true shape of their tax burden. As it is, the Joneses' most hated taxes are those that are new and those that have designated days of reckoning. The stateside Joneses direct their ire at property taxes and time-consuming income taxes. B.C. Jones probably hates these, too, plus the relatively new Canadian value-added tax, the GST.[153]

heavy polluters. But the short- and long-term beneficiaries, if they were organized, could find ways to overcome these forces. Clean businesses in the service and technology industries, for example, employ seven times as many people in the Northwest as do the logging and mining industries.

The biggest obstacle to tax shifting is not likely to be its active opponents but its inactive one: habit. Accustomed to taxes as they are, most citizens are not shopping for fundamental reform. Voters are naturally conservative; they do not want to fix things that are not broken. Existing taxes are the devil they know. Taxes on pollution, traffic, sprawl, and resource consumption are a devil they don't know. Of course, many citizens regarded sales and income taxes as the impractical schemes of wild-eyed dreamers back when customs duties funded our national treasuries.

In the end, a shift will benefit us all: no one gains from a dying landscape and a hobbled economy. All that stands between us and a tax shift is a lot of natural skepticism. Enough leadership, organizing, and public dialogue—and a few crises (real or perceived)—will launch the next tax revolt. Indeed, incipient environmental levies enacted in recent years may be the equivalents of the 14-page trade law amendment that gave birth to the U.S. personal income tax. It all depends what we do next, and how many of us rise to do it.

APPENDIX

Tax and Other Revenue Collected in the Pacific Northwest, 1996 (billions of U.S. and Canadian dollars)

	B.C.	Idaho	Ore.	Wash.	Alaska	Calif.	Mont.
Federal taxes							
Personal income	9.0	2.2	7.2	15.1	1.8	78.1	1.5
Payroll	4.6	1.8	5.5	10.6	1.2	60.9	1.3
Corporate income	1.8	0.8	2.9	5.3	0.5	31.7	0.7
Value-added	2.9	0.0	0.0	0.0	0.0	0.0	0.0
Motor fuels	0.0	0.2	0.4	0.4	0.1	3.3	0.2
Alcohol, tobacco	1.0	0.0	0.1	0.2	0.0	1.1	0.0
Subtotal Can$19.5		$5.0	$16.1	$31.6	$3.6	$175.1	$3.7
State, provincial, and local taxes							
Personal income	5.0	0.8	2.9	0.0	0.0	21.5	0.4
Corporate income	1.8	0.2	0.5	1.6	0.4	5.9	0.1
Sales	2.9	0.6	0.0	5.4	0.1	25.0	0.0
Property	3.2	0.7	2.3	5.7	0.7	20.2	0.8
Environmental	4.9	0.4	0.9	2.6	2.5	9.2	0.4
Other	1.8	0.0	0.7	0.7	0.2	5.2	0.1
Subtotal Can$19.6		$2.7	$7.4	$16.1	$3.9	$87.0	$1.8
Total **Can$39.1**		**$7.7**	**$23.5**	**$47.7**	**$7.5**	**$262.1**	**$5.5**
Per capita Can$10,486		$6,460	$7,320	$8,630	$12,260	$8,220	$6,190
Selected tax rates (state, provincial, and local only)*							
Property tax	0.8%	1.5%	1.3%	1.8%	1.0%	1.0%	2.0%
Sales tax	7.0%	5.0%	0.0%	8.2%	0.4%	7.3%	0.0%
Effective tax on energy	N/A	0.4%	2.1%	6.3%	−0.4%	4.1%	1.6%
Cigarette tax (U.S. cents/pack)	157	28	58	83	100	37	18
Beer tax (U.S. cents/gal.)	10%	45	8	21	85	20	14

* Canadian-to-U.S. conversion at Can$1.40 = U.S.$1.00; energy tax rate for 1993; cigarette tax for 1998. Sources: see note 4.

TAX SHIFT

Estimated Revenue from Tax Shift Scenario, Pacific Northwest, 1996 (millions of U.S. and Canadian dollars)

	B.C.	Idaho	Ore.	Wash.
Labor and capital taxes				
Business taxes	0	0	0	0
Personal income taxes	3,513	388	1,034	0
Retail sales taxes	0	0	0	2,314
Environmental taxes (existing)	4,853	395	901	2,639
Miscellaneous	1,847	16	769	729
Land-value taxes	3,183	718	2,281	5,674
Carbon tax	271	46	110	228
Pollution taxes				
Point sources	2,637*	161	276	790
Farm chemicals	30	224	130	327
Motor vehicles	495	162	373	602
Traffic congestion taxes	700	0	500	1,000
Natural resource taxes				
Water use	N/A	288	150	168
Hydropower	1,414	183	668	1,471
Timber	445	32	115	100
Fish and game	N/A	23	28	27
Minerals	246	40	26	61
Total	Can$19,633	$2,676	$7,361	$16,131

B.C. pollution total is high in part because some U.S. water pollution data are unavailable and because toxic material listings differ between countries. See below for notes and sources.

Details of Tax Shift Scenario

Labor, capital, environmental, and miscellaneous taxes Remainder of all or part of existing taxes.

Land-value taxes We assume a revenue-neutral shift of property taxes onto land values. Revenue is equivalent to

Actual Local, State, and Provincial Revenue, Pacific Northwest, 1996 (millions of U.S. and Canadian dollars)

	B.C.	Idaho	Ore.	Wash.
Labor and capital taxes				
Business taxes	1,781	173	508	1,642
Personal income taxes	4,992	771	2,902	0
Retail sales taxes	2,977	603	0	5,447
Environmental taxes (detailed below)	4,853	395	901	2,639
Miscellaneous	1,847	16	769	729
Property taxes	3,183	718	2,281	5,674
Total	Can$19,633	$2,676	$7,361	$16,131

Existing environmental taxes				
Motor vehicles and fuels	1,174	250	595	1,380
Alcohol and tobacco	1,049	34	210	412
Timber	1,800	0	63	514
Water	268	0	0	0
Minerals	246	1	0	0
Fish and game	18	23	28	27
Electricity	115	3	3	227
Other	185	83	3	79
Subtotal	Can$4,853	$395	$901	$2,639

actual property tax revenue generated in 1996. For data sources, see note 4.

Carbon tax We assume tax rates per ton of carbon (and proportional taxes on other greenhouse gases) of $10 at state or provincial level. (National tax of $100 per ton of carbon not included in tax shift scenario.) Data for 1994, from John C. Ryan, *Over Our Heads: A Local Look at Global Climate* (Seattle: NEW, 1997). Revenue estimates assume a 15 percent reduction in emissions.

Point-source toxic pollution taxes Data on economic costs of toxic emissions essentially nonexistent. Our rate—which averages $16,000 per ton ($8 per pound) but would vary widely depending on pollutant—is four times lower than the $32.35 per pound average water toxics tax used in U.S. Congressional Budget Office, *Reducing the Deficit: Spending and Revenue Options* (Washington, D.C.: 1997; also at *www.cbo.gov*). Toxic emissions data for 1995, from Office of Pollution Prevention and Toxics, *1995 Toxics Release Inventory: State Fact Sheets* (Washington, D.C.: U.S. Environmental Protection Agency [EPA], 1997), and Environment Canada, *National Pollutant Release Inventory Summary Report 1995* (Hull, Quebec: 1997). Revenue estimates assume a 15 percent reduction in emissions.

Other point-source air pollution taxes A number of studies estimate the economic costs of air pollution. Our rates—per ton taxes of $11 for carbon monoxide (CO), $2,400 for oxides of nitrogen (NO_x), $3,200 for particulate matter (PM10), $5,950 for oxides of sulfur (SO_x), and $2,200 for volatile organic compounds (VOCs)—based on estimates from G. E. Bridges and Associates, *Evaluation of External Costs Associated with Natural Gas Use,* vol. 2, Sept. 1991, cited in Transport 2021, *The Cost of Transporting People in the British Columbia Lower Mainland* (Vancouver, B.C.: Greater Vancouver Regional District, 1993). Data for 1995–96 from EPA Region 10 at *www.epa.gov/r10earth/r10.html*

and from Vesna Kontic, *Inventory of Authorized Discharges under the Waste Management Permit Fees Regulation 1994/95–1995/96* (Victoria, B.C.: Ministry of Environment, Lands and Parks, 1996). Revenue estimates assume a 15 percent reduction in emissions.

Other point-source water pollution taxes Data on economic costs of water pollution essentially nonexistent. Our rates—per ton taxes of $1,300 for biological oxygen demand (BOD) and $650 for suspended solids (SS)—based on Congressional Budget Office, *Reducing the Deficit* (cited above), which uses a tax of $1,300 per ton for BOD, and on the relative rates for BOD and SS in use in B.C. We include only data for B.C.; though EPA collects U.S. emissions data, we could not convert them to usable form. Also unavailable were data on nutrients and oil and grease, which, along with BOD and SS, are major nontoxic water pollutants. B.C. data for 1995–96 from Vesna Kontic, *Inventory of Authorized Discharges* (cited above). Revenue estimates assume a 15 percent reduction in emissions.

Farm chemical taxes Data on economic costs of farm chemicals sparse to nonexistent. Our pesticide tax rate—averaging $16,000 per ton but varying widely depending on pesticide—based on David Pimentel et al., "Environmental and Economic Costs of Pesticide Use," *BioScience*, Nov. 1992, who estimate costs of at least $8 billion from the $4 billion spent on the 500,000 tons of pesticides used annually in the United States. Fertilizer tax rate of $75 per ton is approximately half of current U.S. fertilizer prices given in Harold Taylor, Fertilizer Use and Price Statistics,

1960–1993 (Washington, D.C.: Economic Research Service, Dept. of Agriculture, 1994). U.S. pesticide data are non-year-specific estimates for the early 1990s, from Leonard P. Gianessi and James Earl Anderson, *Pesticide Use in Idaho Crop Production* (Washington, D.C.: National Center for Food and Agricultural Policy, 1995), and similar publications for Oregon and Washington. U.S. fertilizer data for 1996 from D. L. Terry and Paul Z. Yu, *Commercial Fertilizers 1996* (Lexington, Ky.: Association of American Plant Food Control Officials, 1996). (Idaho fertilizer use estimated from surrounding states.) B.C. pesticide data for 1995 from Pollution Prevention and Remediation Branch, *Survey of Pesticide Use in British Columbia: 1995* (Victoria, B.C.: Ministry of Environment, Lands and Parks, 1997). B.C. fertilizer data for 1996 from Canadian Fertilizer Institute, *Retail Sales Survey for Western Canada* (Ottawa: 1996). Revenue estimates assume a 15 percent reduction in emissions.

Motor vehicle taxes Tax rates for emissions of CO, NO_x, PM10, SO_x, and VOCs equivalent to those for point sources given above; air toxics ignored. We used PM10 instead of the more-appropriate PM2.5 because PM2.5 inventories were unavailable except for Douglas Lowenthal et al., *CMB Source Apportionment During REVEAL (Regional Visibility Experiment in the Lower Fraser Valley): Final Report* (Victoria: Air Resources Branch, Ministry of Environment, Lands and Parks, 1994). B.C. data for 1990 from Air Resources Branch, *1990 British Columbia Emissions Inventory of Common Air Contaminants* (Victoria, B.C.: Ministry of Environment, Lands and Parks, 1994). U.S. data for 1995 from Emissions Factors Inventory Group, *Emissions Trends Viewer CD 1985–*

1995, version 1.0 (Washington, D.C.: EPA, Sept. 1996). Revenue estimates assume a 15 percent reduction in emissions.

Traffic congestion taxes Figure of $1 billion for Seattle area based on Puget Sound Regional Council, *Metropolitan Transportation Plan* (Seattle: 1995). Estimates for Portland and Vancouver, B.C., based on Seattle figure and metropolitan population comparisons with Seattle.

Water taxes Data on economic costs of water use nonexistent. We use $20 tax per acre-foot, or about $0.06 per thousand gallons. B.C. data unavailable. U.S. data for 1995, from Wayne B. Solley, *Preliminary Estimates of Water Use in the United States, 1995* (Reston, Va.: U.S. Geological Survey, 1997; also at *www.usgs.gov*). Revenue estimates assume a 15 percent reduction in consumption.

Hydropower taxes Data sparse on the economic costs of dams. We use 0.5 cent per kilowatt-hour (kWh). We assume rent capture will bring in another 1 cent per kWh, for a total of 1.5 cents per kWh. Data for 1996 from Statistics Canada, CANSIM (Canadian Socio-Economic Information Management System) database, "Electric Power Statistics in British Columbia" and "Electric Power Statistics in Canada" (*www.statcan.ca*), and from U.S. Dept. of Energy, Energy Information Administration, *Electric Power Annual 1996*, vol. 1 (Washington, D.C., 1997; also at *www.eia.doe.gov*).

Timber taxes We use $20 tax per thousand board feet. U.S. and B.C. data for 1992 from U.S. Forest Service, *USFS Resource Bulletin PNW-RB-202* (Washington, D.C.: 1994).

Fish taxes We assume that rent capture will double existing revenues. For data sources, see note 4.

Minerals We assume that rent capture will double existing revenues in B.C. (sources in note 4). U.S. revenue figures assume 10 percent tax on mineral value, using 1995 data from Bureau of the Census, *Statistical Abstract of the United States 1996* (Washington, D.C.: 1996).

NOTES

1. See Appendix and note 3.
2. David M. Roodman, "Taxation Shifting in Europe," in Lester R. Brown, Michael Renner, and Christopher Flavin, eds., *Vital Signs 1998* (New York: Norton, 1998).
3. Oregon and California families' taxes based on 1997 federal income tax form 1040EZ and Michael P. Ettlinger et al., *Who Pays? A Distributional Analysis of the Tax System in All 50 States* (Washington, D.C.: Citizens for Tax Justice and the Institution on Taxation and Economic Policy, 1996), assuming a median-income non-elderly married couple with one child who receive all income from wages (taxed at 15.3 percent for payroll taxes) and claim all normal exemptions and deductions under federal income tax. B.C. profits tax from note 4c below. B.C. annual pollution and fee rate estimated from 1995–96 data in Vesna Kontic, *Inventory of Authorized Discharges under the Waste Management Permit Fees Regulation 1994/95–1995/96* (Victoria: Ministry of Environment, Lands and Parks, 1996). Washington tax rates from note 4t below. California's timber tax from State Board of Equalization, "California Timber Yield Tax," pamphlet 86 (Sacramento: 1994).
4. The division between labor or capital and resource taxation assumes that 40 percent of property tax revenue comes from the land-value portion of property taxes and that 10 percent of corporate and personal income taxes comes from natural resource income—so-called "rents." Also included in resource taxes are all energy, environmental, and health taxes (details in Appendix). Tax data for the Northwest used in this book are based on conversations with numerous tax administrators throughout the Northwest and North America, and on numerous government publications and Web sites. Most data are for fiscal 1996, though some are for the 1996 calendar year or fiscal 1995.

    Major sources: For B.C. and Canada: (a) B.C. Ministry of Finance and Corporate Relations, *1996 British Columbia Financial and Economic Review* (Victoria: 1996); (b) B.C. Stats, *British*

Columbia Economic Accounts, 1986–1995 (Victoria: 1996); (c) Dept. of Foreign Affairs and International Trade,"Taxation in Canada," from *www.dfait-maeci.gc.ca,* Feb. 26, 1998; (d) Dept. of Finance Canada, *Government of Canada Tax Expenditures 1997* (Ottawa: 1997); (e) Dept. of Finance Canada,"Budget Chart Book 1997," from *www.fin.gc.ca/*, Feb. 26, 1998. Other Web sites are B.C. Stats: *www.bcstats.gov.bc.ca;* B.C. Dept. of Finance: *www.fin.gov.bc.ca;* and Statistics Canada: *www.statcan.ca.* For U.S. federal taxes: (f) Monica E. Friar et al., *The Federal Budget and the States: Fiscal Year 1995* (Washington, D.C.: Office of Sen. Daniel P. Moynihan, U.S. Senate, and Taubman Center for State and Local Government, Harvard Univ., 1996), and Tax Foundation, *Tax Features* and other publications (Washington, D.C.: 1997; also at *www.taxfoundation.org*). For Alaska: (g) Income and Excise Audit Division, *Fiscal Year 1996 Annual Report* (Juneau: Alaska Dept. of Revenue, 1996); (h) Alaska Dept. of Revenue, *Spring 1996 Revenue Sources Book: Forecast and Historical Data* (Juneau: 1996). Web site: *www.revenue.state.ak.us.* For California: (i) California State Board of Equalization, *Annual Report 1995–1996* (Sacramento: 1997; also at *www.boe.ca.gov/*); (j) Dept. of Finance, *Tax Expenditure Report 1997–98* (Sacramento: 1997; also at *www.dof.ca.gov/*). For Idaho: (k) Idaho State Tax Commission, *Annual Report 1996* (Boise: 1997). For Montana: (m) Montana Dept. of Revenue, *Biennial Report 1994–1996* (Helena: 1996; also at *www.mt.gov/ revenue/rev.htm*). For Oregon: (n) Ore. Legislative Revenue Office, *Basic Tax Packet: Research Report #4-97* (Salem: 1997); (p) Budget and Management Division, *State of Oregon 1997–99 Tax Expenditure Report* (Salem: Dept. of Administrative Services, 1997); (q) Ore. Dept. of Revenue,"A Summary of Oregon Taxes" (Salem: Apr. 1995); (r) Ore. Dept. of Revenue, "Monthly Receipt Statement" (Salem: June 1996). Web site: *www.dor.state.or.us/ default.html.* For Washington: (s) Research Division, *Tax Statistics 1996* (Olympia: Dept. of Revenue, 1997); (t) Research Division, *Tax Reference Manual: Information on State and Local Taxes in Washington State* (Olympia: Dept. of Revenue, 1996); (u) Research Division, *Tax Exemptions—1996: A Study of Tax Exemptions, Exclusions, Deductions, Deferrals, Differential Rates, and Credits for Major State and Local Taxes in Washington* (Olympia: Dept. of Revenue, 1995). Web site: *www.wa.gov/DOR/wadorrpt.htm.*

5. Sources in note 4.

6. Deadweight losses are estimated roughly using tax-by-tax computation with average deadweight losses from Dale W. Jorgenson and Kun-Young Yun, "The Excess Burden of Taxation in the United States," *Journal of Accounting, Auditing, and Finance*, fall 1991. Reduction in economic output based on gross regional product of $329 billion from B.C. Stats, "B.C. Business' Economics Accounts," *www.bcstats.gov.bc.ca/data/bus_stat/bcea/tab01. htm*, Jan. 9, 1998, and U.S. Bureau of Economic Analysis, *www.bea.doc.gov/bea/newsrel/gsp7794.txt*, Jan. 9, 1998, assuming 5 percent growth over 1994 gross state product.

7. Estimated 1996 causes of death based on J. Michael McGinnis and William H. Foege, "Actual Causes of Death in the United States," *Journal of the American Medical Association*, Nov. 10, 1993. We applied McGinnis and Foege's percentages of total deaths due alcohol and tobacco and a sum of low estimates for noncardiopulmonary deaths from toxic agents to regional death figures from vital statistics sources including B.C. Vital Statistics Agency, "1996 Annual Report," *www.hlth.gov.bc.ca/vs/stats/annual/1996/index.html*, Jan. 20, 1998; Idaho Center for Vital Statistics and Health Policy, *1996 Annual Summary of Vital Statistics* (Boise: 1997); Ore. Health Division, Center for Health Statistics, *www.ohd.hr.state.or.us/cdpe/chs/cdb96p/tbl1_96p.htm*, Jan. 5, 1998; and Center for Health Statistics, *Washington State Vital Statistics 1996* (Olympia: Dept. of Health, 1997). B.C. Vital Statistics Agency's estimates of smoking- and alcohol-attributable deaths used instead of comparable figures from our estimation.

Cardiopulmonary deaths due to air pollutants from Deborah Shprentz, *Breath-Taking: Premature Mortality Due to Particulate Air Pollution in 239 American Cities* (New York: Natural Resources Defense Council, 1996), with additional data from *www.nrdc.org/nrdcpro/bt/tableGu.html*, Dec. 1997; and Sverre Vedal, *Health Effects of Inhalable Particles: Implications for British Columbia* (Vancouver: B.C. Ministry of Environment, Lands and Parks, 1995; also at *www.env.gov.bc.ca*). Motor vehicle deaths from Greg Hastings, Ore. State Police Dept., Portland, private communication, Jan. 5, 1998; Julie Macdonald, B.C. Vital Statistics Agency, Victoria, private communication, Dec. 23, 1997; Pat Starzik, Wash. Center for Health Statistics, Olympia, private communication,

Jan. 27, 1998; and annual vital statistics reports from Idaho and
Washington.

8. Figures do not add to total because of 800 drunk driving deaths
counted in both alcohol and motor vehicle deaths. Total deaths
from vital statistics series, op. cit. note 7. Deaths of children from
David Hopkins, Ore. Health Division, Center for Health Statistics, Portland, private communication, Jan. 5, 1998, and Tamara
Hogg, Idaho Center for Vital Statistics and Health Policy, Boise,
private communication, Dec. 30, 1997; figure for child deaths
estimates Oregon deaths from 1995 data.

9. John Bartlett, *Familiar Quotations* (Boston: Little, Brown, 1968).

10. The Joneses' personal characteristics drawn from state and pro-
vincial medians (exceptions below). Sources: Edith R. Horner,
ed., *Almanac of the 50 States: Basic Data Profiles with Comparative
Tables*, 1997 ed. (Palo Alto, Calif.: Information Publications, 1997);
George E. Hall and Deirdre A. Gaquin, eds., *1997 County and
City Extra: Annual Metro, City, and County Data Book* (Lanham,
Md.: Bernan Press, 1997); B.C. Stats at *www.bcstats.gov.bc.ca/*; Statistics Canada at *www.statcan.ca*; and Tamara Hogg and Glenda
Larson, Idaho Center for Vital Statistics and Health Policy, Boise,
private communications, Dec. 30, 1997, and Jan. 13, 1998. Joneses'
genders loosely based on regional averages; number of Jones
children is based on average household size, except for B.C.
Jones, who is assumed to have two children because tax and
income figures discussed in Chapter 2 are available only for a
family of four.

11. U.S. data are median household incomes and taxes for non-elderly married couples in 1995 from Ettlinger et al., op. cit. note 3.
B.C. data are for two-income family of four earning Can$55,000
in 1997, which approximates inflation-adjusted median household income for previous years. B.C. tax burden from British Columbia Ministry of Finance and Corporate Relations, *Budget 97:
Reports* (Victoria: 1997; also at *www.fin.gov.bc.ca/*).

12. Colbert quoted in John Steele Gordon, "American Taxation,"
American Heritage, May/June 1996.

13. Tax sources given in note 4. Gross regional product from B.C.
Stats and U.S. Bureau of Economic Analysis, both op. cit. note 6.

14. Revenue code from Gordon, op. cit. note 12, except word count

NOTES 103

from George Will, "Forbes Sees the Presidency As an Entry-
Level Job," *Seattle Post-Intelligencer*, Oct. 8, 1997.

15. Jurisdictions from notes 4a and 4t.
16. Number of tax specialists from Gordon, op. cit. note 12.
17. Philip J. Roberts, *Of Rain and Revenue: The Politics of Income Taxation in the State of Washington, 1862–1940* (Ph.D. dissertation,
Univ. of Washington, Seattle, 1990), and W. Irwin Gillespie, *Tax,
Borrow and Spend: Financing Federal Spending in Canada, 1867–
1990* (Ottawa: Carleton Univ. Press, 1991).
18. Roberts, op. cit. note 17; Gordon, op. cit. note 12.
19. National deadweight losses from Jorgenson and Yun, op. cit.
note 6. State and provincial deadweight losses from Robert
Repetto et al., *Green Fees: How a Tax Shift Can Work for the Environment and the Economy* (Washington, D.C.: World Resources
Institute, 1992).
20. Hours from Arthur B. Little study cited in Lansing Pollock, *The
Free Society* (Boulder, Colo.: Westview Press, 1996). Compliance
from John L. Mikesell, "The American Retail Sales Tax: Con-
siderations on Their Structure, Operations, and Potential As a
Foundation for a Federal Sales Tax," *National Tax Journal*, Mar.
1997, and Matthew N. Murray, "Would Tax Evasion and Tax
Avoidance Undermine a National Retail Sales Tax?" *National
Tax Journal*, Mar. 1997.
21. Roberts, op. cit. note 17.
22. Ibid. Sidney Ratner, "Taxation," in Glenn Porter, ed., *Encyclope-
dia of American Economic History*, vol. 1 (New York: Scribner's, 1980).
23. Gillespie, op. cit. note 17.
24. M. Jeff Hamond et al., *Tax Waste, Not Work: How Changing What
We Tax Can Lead to a Stronger Economy and a Cleaner Environment*
(San Francisco: Redefining Progress, 1997); note 4e. Social Security Trust Fund status from Peter G. Peterson, *Facing Up: How
to Rescue the Economy from Crushing Debt and Restore the American
Dream* (New York: Simon & Schuster, 1993); Canadian Pension
Plan (CPP) changes from *www.cpp-rpc.gc.ca*, Feb. 1998.
25. Jorgenson and Yun, op. cit. note 6. Payroll expenses from Hamond
et al., op. cit. note 24.
26. Tax caps from Tim Beard, Social Security Administration, Seattle Office, private communication, Feb. 24, 1998, and CPP, op.

cit. note 24. Tax burden on families and incidence on wages from Hamond et al., op. cit. note 24; effects on children from U.S. Bureau of the Census, *Measuring the Effects of Benefits and Taxes on Income and Poverty, 1992* (Washington, D.C.: 1993).

27. Gillespie, op. cit. note 17.

28. Roberts, op. cit. note 17; W. Irwin Gillespie, "British Columbia: Government Expenditure, Revenue, and Budget Deficit, 1871–1968," *Canadian Tax Journal*, July/Aug. 1988. General property taxation from Edward T. Howe and Donald J. Reeb, "The Historical Evolution of State and Local Tax Systems," *Social Science Quarterly*, Mar. 1997.

29. Deadweight losses of land-value tax from William Vickrey, "Simplification, Progression, and a Level Playing Field," *Tax Notes*, Nov. 11, 1996; of property taxes from Jorgenson and Yun, op. cit. note 6. (Deadweight losses from buildings estimated, after Jorgenson and Yun, assuming that building values are typically twice land values.)

30. Dick Netzer, "What Do We Need to Know about Land Value Taxation?" Founder's Day Lecture, Lincoln Institute of Land Policy, Sept. 22, 1997, and Cliff Cobb, *Fiscal Policy for a Sustainable California Economy*, unpublished report prepared for Redefining Progress, San Francisco, 1995.

31. Cobb, op. cit. note 30; C. Lowell Harriss, "Property Taxation: What's Good and What's Bad," *Challenge: The Magazine of Economic Affairs*, Sept./Oct. 1973.

32. Netzer, op. cit. note 30.

33. Roberts, op. cit. note 17.

34. Ibid. Voting history from note 4n.

35. Jorgenson and Yun, op. cit. note 6.

36. Cobb, op. cit. note 30; Ettlinger et al., op. cit. note 3.

37. Sources in note 4.

38. Roberts, op. cit. note 17.

39. James E. Hartley, Steven M. Sheffrin, and J. David Vasche, "Reform During Crisis: The Transformation of California's Fiscal System During the Great Depression," *Journal of Economic History*, Sept. 1996.

40. Leonard J. Arrington, *History of Idaho*, vol. 2 (Moscow, Idaho: Univ. of Idaho Press, 1994). Sales tax from College of Social

Sciences and Public Affairs, Boise State Univ., "History of Tax Policy in Idaho," *Idaho Issues*, spring 1997.

41. See Appendix and note 4.

42. Vickrey, op. cit. note 29; Jorgenson and Yun, op. cit. note 6.

43. Vickrey, op. cit. note 29; Richard M. Bird, *Why Tax Corporations? Working Paper 96-2* (Ottawa: Technical Committee on Business Taxation, Dept. of Finance, 1996; also at *www.fin.gc.ca/*).

44. See, for example, U.S. Congress, Joint Committee on Taxation, "Estimates of Federal Tax Expenditures for Fiscal Years 1997–2001," Washington, D.C., Nov. 26, 1996. Washington from note 4t.

45. Vickrey, op. cit. note 29.

46. B.C. from J. Harvey Perry, *Taxes, Tariffs, and Subsidies: A History of Canadian Fiscal Development* (Toronto: Canadian Tax Foundation and Univ. of Toronto Press, 1955). Alaska from Claus-M. Naske and Herman E. Slotnick, *Alaska: A History of the 49th State*, 2d ed. (Norman, Okla.: Univ. of Oklahoma Press, 1987).

47. Notes 4p and 4u.

48. Idaho from Arrington, op. cit. note 40. Property and income tax revenue effects from Michael J. Boskin, "Some Neglected Economic Factors behind Recent Tax and Spending Limitation Movements," *National Tax Journal* (suppl.), June 1979. Windfall to median-home-value property owner from Stephen J. DeCanio, "Proposition 13 and the Failure of Economic Politics," *National Tax Journal* (suppl.), June 1979. Washington from note 4t.

49. Oregon from note 4n. California from *Daily Tax Reporter*, Nov. 7, 1996. Washington from note 4t. Oregon ballots from "Ballot Measure Endorsements," *Willamette Week*, Oct. 15, 1997.

50. Howe and Reeb, op. cit. note 28.

51. Ettlinger et al., op. cit. note 3. Figure 1 based on non-elderly married couples because they allow ready comparisons, while dissimilar household types do not. Data corrected for deductibility of certain state and local taxes on federal income tax returns.

52. DRI/McGraw-Hill, *The Tax Burden on America's Beer Drinkers*, June 1996, at *issues.anheuser-busch.com/docs/taxburd.htm*, Jan. 20, 1998.

53. Sources and assumptions in notes 3 and 11. Totals do not include federal excise taxes.

54. John C. Ryan, *Over Our Heads: A Local Look at Global Climate* (Seattle: NEW, 1997).

55. Roger C. Dower and Mary Beth Zimmerman, *The Right Climate for Carbon Taxes: Creating Economic Incentives to Protect the Atmosphere* (Washington, D.C.: World Resources Institute, 1992).
56. Hamond et al., op. cit. note 24.
57. Greenhouse gas emissions from Ryan, op. cit. note 54. Payroll tax revenues from sources listed in note 4; household's savings equal a 27.25 percent reduction in the payroll taxes paid by average Northwest families. Sources in notes 3 and 11. Price impacts estimated on the basis of fuel prices from U.S. Dept. of Energy, Energy Information Administration, "Monthly Energy Review," *ftp://ftp.eia.doe.gov/pub/energy.overview/monthly.energy/ mer9–10*, Mar. 16, 1997; carbon contents from Gregg Marland, "Carbon Dioxide Emission Rates for Conventional and Synthetic Fuels," *Energy,* vol. 8, no. 12 (1983); and David M. Roodman, Worldwatch Institute, Washington, D.C., private communication, Feb. 25, 1998.
58. Emissions from Ryan, op. cit. note 54.
59. Revenue figure assumes a 15 percent reduction in emissions below 1994 levels; see note 57 for sources.
60. Sources detailed in Appendix.
61. Agricultural impact from Steve Butkus, *1998 Washington State Water Quality Assessment: Section 305(b) Report* (Olympia: Dept. of Ecology, 1997), and Tim Palmer, *The Snake River: Window to the West* (Washington, D.C.: Island Press, 1991).
62. Theo Colborn et al., *Our Stolen Future: Are We Threatening Our Fertility, Intelligence, and Survival?—A Scientific Detective Story* (New York: Dutton, 1996), and Shanna H. Swan et al., "Have Sperm Densities Declined? A Reanalysis of Global Trend Data," *Environmental Health Perspectives,* Nov. 1997.
63. U.S. cancer rates from Sandra Steingraber, *Living Downstream: An Ecologist Looks at Cancer and the Environment* (New York: Addison-Wesley, 1997); Ries Lag et al., eds., *SEER Cancer Statistics Review, 1973–1994* (Bethesda, Md.: National Cancer Institute, 1997; also at *www.nci.nih.gov*); and John Cushman, "U.S. Reshaping Cancer Strategy As Incidence in Children Rises," *New York Times,* Sept. 29, 1997. Canadian rates from National Cancer Institute of Canada, *Canadian Cancer Statistics 1997* (Toronto: 1997).
64. Steingraber, op. cit. note 63; Colborn et al., op. cit. note 62; and John Wargo, *Our Children's Toxic Legacy: How Science and Law Fail*

to Protect Us from Pesticides (New Haven, Conn.: Yale Univ. Press, 1996).

65. Wargo, op. cit. note 64. Apple residues from U.S. Environmental Protection Agency (EPA) and Oregon State Univ., National Pesticide Telecommunications Network, *ace.ace.orst.edu/info/nptn*, Jan. 1998.

66. European experience from David M. Roodman, *Getting the Signals Right: Tax Reform to Protect the Environment and the Economy* (Washington, D.C.: Worldwatch Institute, 1997), and J. Schut, "Twenty-Five Years of Waste Water Management in the Netherlands—An Industrial View," *Water Science and Technology*, vol. 32, no. 11 (1995). U.S. states from Point Source Management Section, *A Summary of Other States' Wastewater Discharge Permit Fees* (Olympia: Dept. of Ecology, 1993), and National Conference of State Legislatures, *Summary of State Wastewater Discharge Permit Fees (NPDES) FY 1993 and FY 1994* (Denver, Colo.: 1993). CFCs from William S. Pease et al., *Taxing Pesticides to Fund Environmental Protection and Integrated Pest Management* (Berkeley: Calif. Policy Seminar, 1996).

67. U.S. air pollution fees from Joan Cabreza, Air Permits Team Leader, EPA Region 10, Seattle, private communication, Dec. 8, 1997. U.S. water pollution charges from Point Source Management Section and National Conference of State Legislatures, both op. cit. note 66. Charges in B.C. from Kontic, op. cit. note 3.

68. Roodman, op. cit. note 66.

69. Roodman, op. cit. note 66, and EPA's SO$_2$ Emissions Trading Program, *www.epa.gov/acidrain/trading.html*, Jan. 20, 1998.

70. Gail North, Wisconsin Dept. of Natural Resources, Madison, Wis., private communication, Jan. 12, 1998.

71. Sources detailed in Appendix.

72. "Behind America's Small-Business Success Story," *Economist*, Dec. 13, 1997.

73. Washington study from Dan Wrye, Alternative Strategies Unit, Wash. Dept. of Ecology, Olympia, private communications, Nov. 1997. Toxic polluters from Office of Pollution Prevention and Toxics, *1995 Toxics Release Inventory State Fact Sheets* (Washington, D.C.: EPA, 1997). Chlorine from Maureen Smith, *The U.S. Paper Industry and Sustainable Production: An Argument for Restructuring* (Cambridge, Mass.: MIT Press, 1997).

74. Sewer systems from Glenn Bohn, "Sewage Plant, Pulp Mill on
     Sinners' List Again," *Vancouver Sun*, Sept. 14, 1994, and Kathy
     George, "A Rising Tide of Pollution," *Seattle Post-Intelligencer*,
     Dec. 3, 1997. Centralia from C. S. Glantz et al., *Air Quality Analysis
     and Related Risk Assessment for the Bonneville Power Administration's
     Resource Program Environmental Impact Statement* (Richland, Wash.:
     Pacific Northwest Laboratory, 1992). Mining from "Toxics Re-
     lease Inventory Expanded to Cover Seven New Industries,"
     Environmental Science and Technology, June 1997, and Bruce Selcraig,
     "An Off-the-Books Polluter," *High Country News*, Sept. 16, 1996,
     also at *www.hcn.org*, Jan. 1998. Factory farms from EPA, "Con-
     centrated Animal Feeding Operations (CAFOs) Requirements,"
     earth2.epa.gov/oeca/aglaws/lawspgb.html, Jan. 1998.
75. Michael E. Porter, "America's Green Strategy," *Scientific Ameri-
     can*, Apr. 1991. Case studies from Curtis A. Moore, "Down
     Germany's Road to a Clean Tomorrow," *International Wildlife*,
     Sept./Oct. 1992; Rolf Golombek and Arvid Raknerud, "Do
     Environmental Standards Harm Manufacturing Employment?"
     Scandinavian Journal of Economics, Mar. 1997; Joseph J. Romm,
     *Lean and Clean Management: How to Boost Profits and Productivity
     by Reducing Pollution* (New York: Kodansha America, 1994); and
     Eban Goodstein and Hart Hodges, "Polluted Data," *American
     Prospect*, Nov./Dec. 1997, also at *www.epn.org/prospect.html*.
76. National Research Council, *Soil and Water Quality: An Agenda for
     Agriculture* (Washington, D.C.: National Academy Press, 1993).
     Data for specific states from Butkus and Palmer, both op. cit.
     note 61; Water Quality and Remediation Division, *1996 Water
     Quality Status Report* (Boise, Idaho: Division of Environmental
     Quality, 1997); and Dept. of Environmental Quality, *Oregon's
     1994 Water Quality Status Assessment Report* (Portland: 1994).
     Groundwater contamination from S. Stewart et al., *The State of
     Our Groundwater: A Report on Documented Contamination in Wash-
     ington* (Seattle: Washington Toxics Coalition and Washington
     State Univ. Cooperative Extension, 1994). Cancer link from
     Steingraber, op. cit. note 63.
77. David Pimentel et al., "Environmental and Economic Costs of
     Pesticide Use," *BioScience*, Nov. 1992.
78. Duff Wilson, "Fear in the Fields," *Seattle Times*, July 3–20, 1997,

NOTES 109

also at *www.seattletimes.com*. Pesticide regulation from Wargo, op. cit. note 64.

79. Anne Weinberg, "Reducing Agricultural Pesticide Use in Sweden," *Journal of Soil and Water Conservation*, Nov./Dec. 1990, and sources detailed in Appendix.

80. William Pease et. al., *Pesticide Use in California: Strategies for Reducing Environmental Health Impacts* (Berkeley: Calif. Policy Seminar, 1996) and private communications with Beth Williams, Agrochemical Specialist, Idaho Dept. of Agriculture, Oct. 14, 1997; Hersh Pendell, Agricultural Specialist, Ore. Dept. of Agriculture, Oct. 14, 1997; Jim Sandeno, Supervisor, Pesticide Regulatory Unit, Ore. Dept. of Agriculture, Oct. 17, 1997; Ali Kashani, Feed and Fertilizer Program Administrator, Pesticide Management Divison, Wash. Dept. of Agriculture, Oct. 15, 1997; and Joel Kangiser, Registration and Minor Crop Program Coordinator, Pesticide Management Divison, Wash. Dept. of Agriculture, Oct. 16, 1997.

81. Note 4u.

82. Jane Malme, "Preferential Property Tax Treatment of Land," Lincoln Institute of Land Policy, Cambridge, Mass., 1993; Julian K. Greenwood and Jennifer A. Whybrow, "Property Tax Treatment of Agricultural and Forestland in Canada: Implications for Land Use Policy," *Property Tax Journal*, June 1992. Oregon from note 4p. Value of tax breaks from sources in note 4.

83. Marty Trillhaase, "Farm Tax Break Abused, Critics Say," *Idaho Statesman*, Mar. 28, 1996. Greenwood and Whybrow, op. cit. note 82.

84. David Pimentel et al., "Environmental and Economic Impacts of Reducing U.S. Agricultural Pesticide Use," in David Pimentel and Hugh Lehman, eds., *The Pesticide Question: Environment, Economics, and Ethics* (New York: Routledge, Chapman & Hall, 1993). Netherlands from Michael E. Porter and Claas van der Linde, "Green and Competitive: Ending the Stalemate," *Harvard Business Review*, Sept./Oct. 1995.

85. Sources detailed in Appendix.

86. Shprentz, op. cit. note 7, and Vedal, op. cit. note 7.

87. Shprentz, op. cit. note 7. Number of motor vehicles from Federal Highway Administration (FHWA), *1995 Highway Statistics* (Washington, D.C.: 1996; also at *www.bts.gov*), and B.C. Stats,

"Quick Facts about British Columbia," *www.bcstats.gov.bc.ca/data/ QF_econo.htm,* Dec. 31, 1997. Sources for air pollution data detailed in Appendix. Evaporation from solvents accounts for about one-quarter of emissions of volatile organic compounds (VOCs) in metropolitan areas. Though not discussed in this book, a tax on solvents' VOC content would encourage companies to use and develop less polluting solvents.

88. Note 4u.

89. Washington from note 4u. U.S. Congress, Joint Committee on Taxation, *Present Law and Background Information on Federal Transportation Excise Taxes and Trust Fund Expenditure Programs* (Washington, D.C.: U.S. Government Printing Office, 1996). Earmarking of fuel-tax revenue, generous treatment of fuel taxes, and negative effective tax rate on motor fuels from Alliance to Save Energy, *State and Local Taxation: Energy Policy by Accident* (Washington, D.C.: 1994), and FHWA, op. cit. note 87. State general tax revenues spent on roads from John C. Ryan, *Hazardous Handouts: Taxpayer Subsidies to Environmental Degradation* (Seattle: NEW, 1995).

90. Parking exemption estimated from Joint Committee on Taxation, op. cit. note 44. Subsidies from Todd Litman, *Transportation Cost Analysis* (Victoria: Victoria Transport Policy Institute, 1995), and Transport 2021, *The Cost of Transporting People in the British Columbia Lower Mainland* (Vancouver: Greater Vancouver Regional District, 1993).

91. Keith Bradsher, "U.S. Auto Makers Showing Interest in Fuel Efficiency," *New York Times,* Jan. 5, 1998.

92. Sources detailed in Appendix. Assumes 11 million vehicles in the Northwest, from note 87.

93. Shprentz, op. cit. note 7; Todd Litman, "Distance-Based Vehicle Insurance as a TDM Strategy," *Transportation Quarterly,* summer 1997.

94. M. J. Heimrich et al., "Electrically Heated Catalysts for Cold-Start Emission Control of Gasoline- and Methanol-Fueled Vehicles," *Journal of Engineering for Gas Turbines and Power,* July 1992, and Lily Whiteman, "A Meeting with the Dynamometer," *EPA Journal,* July/Aug. 1992. Congestion from "No Room, No Room," *Economist,* Dec. 6, 1997.

95. Tony Brasil, Air Resources Engineer, California Air Resources Board, Sacramento, private communication, Jan. 30, 1998, and

John Raymond, Planner, Air Quality Division, Wash. Dept. of Ecology, Olympia, private communication, Jan. 29, 1998.

96. Brett C. Singer and Robert A. Harley, "A Fuel-Based Motor Vehicle Inventory," *Journal of the Air and Waste Management Association*, June 1996, and Yi Zhang et al., "Enhancement of Remote Sensing for Mobile Source Nitric Oxide," *Journal of the Air and Waste Management Association*, Jan. 1996.

97. California's DRIVE+ program from Cobb, op. cit. note 30. Cost differences from Clean Vehicles and Fuels Program, *Protecting the Air We Breathe—A British Columbia Action Plan for Cleaner Air* (Victoria: Ministry of Environment, Lands and Parks, 1995; also at *www.env.gov.bc.ca*), and Keith Bradsher, "Auto Makers Plan Cuts in Emissions of Sport Vehicles," *New York Times*, Jan. 6, 1998.

98. Mike Baker, Air Resources Engineer, California Air Resources Board, Sacramento, private communication, Jan. 23, 1998.

99. David L. Schrank and Timothy J. Lomax, *Urban Roadway Congestion, 1982 to 1994* (College Station, Tex.: Texas Transportation Institute, 1997; also at *tti.tamu.edu/mobility*). Survey results from Eric Pryne, "Growth, Traffic Spoiling Region, Residents Fear," *Seattle Times*, Sept. 21, 1997, and Greater Vancouver Regional District (GVRD), *Great Vancouver Regional Transportation Demand Management Project: Final Report* (Vancouver, B.C.: 1996).

100. Anthony Downs, "The Law of Peak-Hour Expressway Congestion," *Traffic Quarterly* (now *Transportation Quarterly*), July 1962.

101. Miles of roadway from John C. Ryan, "Roads Take Toll on Salmon, Grizzlies, Taxpayers," *NEW Indicator*, Dec. 1995. Portland estimates from Metro, "How Do We Get from Here to There?" *2040 News*, fall 1997/winter 1998, also at *www.metro-region.org*, and Metro, *Draft Alternatives Analysis Findings* (Portland: 1997).

102. Metro, *Interim Federal Regional Transportation Plan* (Portland: 1995), and Puget Sound Regional Council (PSRC), *1995 Metropolitan Transportation Plan* (Seattle: 1995).

103. PSRC, op. cit. note 102; PSRC, "Regional Transportation System Action Strategy: Six-Year Action Strategy" Jan. 1998; Metro, *Draft Alternatives Analysis Findings*, op. cit. note 101; Transport 2021, *A Long-Range Transportation Plan for Greater Vancouver* (Burnaby, B.C.: GVRD and Province of British Columbia, 1993).

104. Toll collection technology from "No Room, No Room," op. cit. note 94. See Appendix for revenue estimates.

105. Catherine Bowman, "Riders Find Few Hitches with Casual Carpools," *San Francisco Chronicle*, July 22, 1996, and Marcela Kogan, "Slugs and Body Snatchers," *Government Executive*, June 1997, also at *www.govexec.com*.

106. Vancouver plan from Transport 2021, op. cit. note 103. Portland pilot project from Metro, "Traffic Relief Options Study News," fall 1997. Route 91 from "No Room, No Room," op. cit. note 94.

107. "No. Room, No Room," op. cit. note 94.

108. Michael Cameron, *Efficiency and Fairness on the Road: Strategies for Unsnarling Traffic in Southern California* (Oakland, Calif.: Environmental Defense Fund, 1994), and Thomas Higgins, "Congestion Pricing: Public Polling Perspectives," *Transportation Quarterly*, spring 1997.

109. PSRC, "Regional Transportation System Action Strategy," op. cit. note 103, and PSRC, op. cit. note 102.

110. Harriss, op. cit. note 31, and Vickrey, op. cit. note 29. Pennsylvania from Wallace E. Oates and Robert M. Schwab, "The Impact of Urban Land Taxation: The Pittsburgh Experience," *National Tax Journal*, Mar. 1997. Other places from Thomas A. Gihring, "Incentive Property Taxation in Vancouver, Washington," Public Finance Research Center, Olympia, Nov. 1996, and Cobb, op. cit. note 30.

111. Cobb, op. cit. note 30.

112. Share of materials used in buildings from David M. Roodman and Nicholas Lenssen, *A Building Revolution: How Ecology and Health Concerns Are Transforming Construction* (Washington, D.C.: Worldwatch Institute, 1995). Vacation homes from Carlyn E. Orians and Marina Skumanich, "The Population-Environment Connection: What Does It Mean for Environmental Policy?" Battelle Seattle Research Center, Dec. 1995.

113. Joint Committee on Taxation, op. cit. note 44. Low-income housing spending from Jason DeParle, "Slamming the Door," *New York Times Magazine*, Oct. 20, 1996.

114. Notes 4m and 4p.

115. Notes 4a and 4d.

116. Thomas A. Gihring, "Converting from a Single Rate to a Differential Rate Property Tax: Resulting Changes in Tax Burden among Land Use Classes in King County, Washington," paper presented at the Pacific Northwest Regional Economic Con-

ference, Seattle, Apr. 28–30, 1994. B.C. land and building values from B.C. Assessment Authority, unpublished data, 1995, and B.C. Assessment Authority, *1993 Annual Report* (Victoria: 1994).

117. King County growth and housing price spiral from Gihring, op. cit. note 116. Rogers quoted in Cobb, op. cit. note 30.

118. Harriss, op. cit. note 31; Cobb, op. cit. note 30.

119. Thomas Gihring, Thomas A. Gihring Planning, Seattle, private communication, Jan. 23 1997; Linda Keene, "Stubborn Land Mogul's Legacy: A Nicer Downtown," *Seattle Times*, July 3, 1996.

120. King County vacant and underused lots from Thomas Gihring, Thomas A. Gihring Planning, Seattle, private communication, Jan. 26, 1998, based on data from King County Assessor's Office. Dramatically underused lots defined as those where the assessed value of buildings and other improvements is less than one-third the parcel's total value. Seattle zoning capacity from City of Seattle, "Mayor's Recommended Comprehensive Plan," Mar. 1994. Clark County from Gihring, op. cit. note 110.

121. Thomas A. Gihring and James McIntire, "Equity, Land Use, and Resource Land Impacts of Land Value Taxation in Washington State," draft paper prepared for Lincoln Institute of Land Policy, Cambridge, Mass., 1998.

122. Gihring, op. cit. notes 110 and 116.

123. Cobb, op. cit. note 30.

124. Vickrey, op. cit. note 29.

125. Environmental impacts of extractive industries from, among others, Alan Thein Durning, *How Much Is Enough?* (New York: Norton, 1992).

126. Ryan, op. cit. note 89.

127. See Appendix and note 4.

128. B.C. from Policy and Legislation Services, *Grazing Fees and Irrigation Rates: British Columbia and Competing Provinces and States* (Victoria: Ministry of Agriculture, Fisheries and Food, Dec. 1994). U.S. water consumption from Wayne B. Solley, *Preliminary Estimates of Water Use in the United States, 1995* (Reston, Va.: U.S. Geological Survey, 1997; also at *www.usgs.gov*). Idaho sales tax revenue from note 4k.

129. Irrigation from Solley, op. cit. note 128.

130. Price comparisons estimated from Jeff Allen, "Liquid Assets: The Potential of Water Use Fees," draft paper prepared for Calif.

Senate Office of Research, Sacramento, 1992, and, for Idaho potatoes, from John C. Ryan and Alan Thein Durning, *Stuff: The Secret Lives of Everyday Things* (Seattle: NEW, 1997).

131. Power prices from Ryan, op. cit. note 89. Other sources detailed in Appendix.

132. Federal tax breaks from Joint Committee on Taxation, op. cit. note 44. Montana from Alliance to Save Energy, op. cit. note 89.

133. Alliance to Save Energy, op. cit. note 89.

134. Proportion of North American hydropower from sources detailed in Appendix. Alaska from note 4h.

135. Sources detailed in Appendix.

136. Canadian logging tax from notes 4a and 4d. Timber taxes in Northwest states from sources in note 4 and Calif. State Board of Equalization, op. cit. note 3.

137. Montana timber taxation estimated from note 4m. Oregon from Joint Interim Committee on Revenue and School Finance, Subcommittee on Timber Taxation, "Report of the Subcommittee on Timber Taxation," Legislative Revenue Office, Salem, Ore., Feb. 23, 1993.

138. B.C. from Greenwood and Whybrow, op. cit. note 82. Impacts from Malme, op. cit. note 82. Revenues lost from notes 4p and 4u.

139. National expensing of timber-growing costs from Joint Committee on Taxation, op. cit. note 44. Oregon and Montana from notes 4p and 4m.

140. B.C. timber royalty earnings for fiscal year 1995–96 from note 4a; U.S. timber sale losses, for fiscal year 1996, from the Wilderness Society, *www.wilderness.org*, Feb. 23, 1998.

141. Fishing revenues from sources in note 4. Price of fishing license from Anthony DePalma, "On a Menu of Despair, Salmon Is Just the Starter," *New York Times*, Feb. 6, 1998.

142. Revenue sources listed in note 4.

143. Mine production from Bureau of the Census, *Statistical Abstract of the United States: 1996* (Washington, D.C.: 1996).

144. Sources detailed in Appendix and note 4.

145. See Appendix. Federal carbon tax of $100 per ton of carbon dioxide is ten times state and provincial rate of $10 per ton.

146. Danish tax shift from Roodman, op. cit. note 2.

147. Estimates of economic gains from tax shift probably conservative; derived by applying estimated deadweight losses to the tax

shift scenario in Appendix. We used same deadweight loss values for capital and labor taxes as in calculation described in note 6,
from Jorgenson and Yun, op. cit. note 6. We assumed no deadweight losses from land-value taxes, traffic taxes, or taxes on
resource rents, and we assumed, conservatively, that half of revenues from resource consumption taxes would come from taxes
on rents. Environmental taxes, because they reduce environmental costs in the economy, generally cause much smaller deadweight losses than do conventional taxes. Still, we assumed conservatively that pollution taxes and price-changing resource taxes
have deadweight losses as high as existing sales taxes and that
carbon taxes have deadweight losses as high as payroll taxes.

148. John C. Ryan, "Northwest Employment Depends Less on Timber and Mining," *NEW Indicator*, Nov. 1994.

149. Alliance to Save Energy, op. cit. note 89. Washington from note 4t.

150. Forest Service and counties from Randal O'Toole, "1992
TSPIRS Recalculations," *Forest Watch* (Cascade Holistic Economic Consultants, Oak Grove, Ore.), Apr./May 1993.

151. Urban and rural designations for the Joneses based on proportion of metropolitan residents, from the U.S. Census Bureau,
www.census.gov, Jan. 1998. Car preferences based on registered
passenger vehicle data for the Pacific and Mountain regions,
given in Deebe Ferris, ed., *Ward's 1995 Automotive Yearbook*,
57th ed. (Southfield, Mich.: Intertec Publishing, 1995). Employment from Ryan, op. cit. note 148.

152. Quoted in Gordon, op. cit. note 12.

153. U.S. Advisory Commission on Intergovernmental Relations,
Changing Public Attitudes on Governments and Taxes, 1994 (Wash-
ington, D.C.: 1994), and JuNelle Harris, "Idahoans Say Growth
Is Top Concern," *Idaho Statesman*, July 25, 1997.

Alan Thein Durning is founder and executive director of Northwest Environment Watch and author of award-winning books such as *This Place on Earth* and *How Much Is Enough?* Formerly senior researcher at Worldwatch Institute, he lectures widely and lives with his wife and children in Seattle.

Yoram Bauman is a former research intern at Northwest Environment Watch and a graduate of Reed College in Portland, Oregon. His acceptance to the graduate program in economics at the University of Washington in Seattle foiled his plan to move to the Caribbean tax haven of Trinidad and Tobago.

Northwest Environment Watch (NEW) is an independent, not-for-profit research and communication center in Seattle, Washington. Its mission is to promote a sustainable economy and way of life throughout the Pacific Northwest—the biological region stretching from southeast Alaska to northern California and from the Pacific Ocean to the crest of the Rockies.